# WORLD WAR II

## *An Airman Remembers*

JOHN PATTERSON

Published by

GSPH GENERAL STORE PUBLISHING HOUSE

Box 28, 1694B Burnstown Road
Burnstown, Ontario, Canada K0J 1G0
Telephone (613) 432-7697 or 1-800-465-6072

ISBN 1-894263-31-6
Printed and bound in Canada

Layout and cover design by Leanne Enright
Printing by Custom Printers of Renfrew Ltd.



Canadian Cataloguing in Publication Data

Patterson, John, 1921-
World War II: an airman remembers

Includes bibliographical references.
ISBN 1-894263-31-6

1. Patterson, John, 1921- 2. World War, 1939-1945–Personal narratives, Canadian. 3. World War, 1939-1945–Aerial operations, Canadian. 4. Canada. Royal Canadian Air Force–Biography. I. Title.

D811.P375 2000 940.54’4971’092 C00-901507-8

## *ACKNOWLEDGEMENTS*

I would like to acknowledge the help I received from Susan Code and Tom McCool, both of whom provided editorial guidance and advice. I am particularly indebted to Tom for his encouragement. In addition I am appreciative of the help provided by Terry Goodwin, my pilot on 61 Squadron, Bomber Command, and Tom Jones, our tail gunner.

# PREFACE

This is not a spectacular story. It is not a story that you will want to read from beginning to end in one sitting. It is just my story of my service in the Royal Canadian Air Force during World War II. It is largely based on a diary in which I never failed to make an entry of four to six lines from the day I joined the Air Force (December 7, 1940) to the day (September 20, 1945) when I was informed my services were no longer required. Other sources I have used in my discourse from time to time include my letters to my parents, my flying log book, and articles that I wrote occasionally, perhaps hoping they would be published. But except for one letter to a newspaper, they never were. Possibly when you read them you will understand why. I looked at life differently then than I do now. Solutions to the problems facing Canada and the world came easier to me. Usually they were either black or white. Few were in grey areas.

While on operational flying with my first squadron, the chances of surviving were not good. I, like most of my colleagues, nonetheless continued to look on life positively. I believe my letters home and the articles I wrote reflected that feeling for the most part, but I will leave the final conclusion to you, the reader. It was an extraordinary life we led, not an easy one, but we carried on. What choice did we have?

# CONTENTS

# CHAPTER I

## *Introduction to Life in the Royal Canadian Air Force*

It was early December 1940, when our postman left a letter in the roadside mailbox at my parents' farm near Bobcaygeon, Ontario, telling me that I had been accepted as an aircrew trainee.

I had passed the first hurdle, a medical examination and an interview I had had a few weeks previously. As a consequence, a few days later on Thursday, December 6, a cold and bright day, Laurence Oliver, a high school classmate, and I held up our right arms and stuck out our thumbs to begin hitchhiking to Toronto.

After spending the night sharing a bed with my brother, Harold, who at the time was boarding in a Toronto rooming house, I reported for a medical recheck. It was a slow process; there were many other young men waiting their turn. Finally, after receiving the good news that I was fit for training as pilot or observer, I made my way to the Manning Poole at the exhibition grounds, which was to be my home for the next few weeks. As stated in my diary,

*Had supper. The clatter of dishes was terrific. Found my bunk and fixed it up for my first night with the RCAF. Was agreeably impressed.*

I may have been impressed, but many of my mates were not. Having been brought up on farms in Saskatchewan and Ontario in the midst of the Depression, my expectations were not high. So, even if I had to share a bunk bed and I was surrounded by many other bunk beds in the cattle barn, I did not grumble. Still, if I had I had to stay there for a long period, I am sure, like many of my mates, I, too, would have complained.

Tuesday, December 11, was an exciting day; many of my colleagues and I were given uniforms. It took a long time before I was able to find one that fitted me satisfactorily. Now, I felt there was no turning back; I was in the air force. Our uniforms were left with the tailors to have the eagle emblem sewn on the shoulders of our jackets and greatcoats. Unfortunately my coat *went missing*; it may have been stolen. In any case, it was never found and finally after telling me that I would have to buy one, I was loaned one that over time became a permanent loan. At least I was never asked to pay for it.

Life at the Manning Depot while not exciting was not dull either. One recruit, whose bunk was near mine, went insane and was removed by the security police. We had a lot of drill practice–learning to march with our shoulders back, our heads up and our arms and feet moving in unison. I wondered what marching had to do with flying. Perhaps it was to teach us how to function as a team or maybe it was just to keep us occupied and to exercise our bodies while our superiors were considering various postings for us. Besides drill, we were given rifle practice but, worst of all, many of us had to help the cooks. I remember having to peel baskets of potatoes for several hours. There were other activities, as noted in my diary entry for Saturday, December 15.

*Every man was asked to take part in some sport. We were to play rugby on a cement floor; impossible. In the afternoon, we moved 78 bunks and 156 mattresses.*

We lined up for vaccinations and "short arm" inspections, which presumably were to check for venereal disease; we attended lectures on discipline, on health, particularly as to how, heaven forbid, we should protect ourselves should we allow ourselves to succumb to the charms of a member of the opposite sex.

Two days' leave at Christmas. How generous of the air force! But enough time for some of us to go home. Hitchhiking on the 24th was good, perhaps because I was in uniform. Unfortunately, I had to report back on Christmas day and so left home in the early evening. On December 28, after having been transferred to the 16th Security Guard, we found ourselves on the train for Picton, Ontario. Although Picton is only about 120 miles east of Toronto, the train journey took seven hours. Obviously other trains had priority over ours. I was learning that patience in the armed forces was important. Still I was being paid, not very much, but more than I had ever received over an extended period, probably around $1.30 a day. My first pay was $10, which I received on December 14 after being in the air force seven days.

Guard duty at the Picton Airport hangars and the town reservoir was routine. Fortunately, our stay at Picton was for short time. My comrades were continually complaining about the food we were served and the cooks were intoxicated almost every evening. Consequently, we were pleased to be informed on January 8, 1941, that we were on draft for Dartmouth, Nova Scotia. Three days later, after I had been given 24 hours off duty to visit relatives in Toronto, other members of the 16th Security Guard and I climbed aboard a train bound for Halifax. Following our overnight stay in the YMCA in Halifax on January 12, we arrived at the Darmouth airport, which was to be our home for the next three months. It was in the harbour where for the first time I saw a battleship and a large two-engine amphibian aircraft. I found out later that it was a Stranraer, and I was to have my second flight in it, having had my first flight in a Hudson transport on January 21. Sometime later I had my third flight, this time in a Digby bomber.

Waiting for a ride into Halifax

On these flights during which I was either the only passenger or accompanied by one of my mates, no effort was made on the part of the crew to arouse our interest in flying. We were not invited into the cockpit; we were just told to sit in the back of the aircraft. The flights were a disappointment to me; I had hoped that the crews would give us some encouragement to realize our dreams of someday being a member of aircrew as they were.

The Hudson and Stranraer aircraft deserve a footnote in Canadian aviation history. A few Stranraer aircraft were among the 93 aircraft the RCAF had purchased in 1939 just prior to the war. They had been built in the Vicker's plant in Montreal to be used on coastal patrols. The Hudson's claim to glory, as far as Canadian aviation history is concerned, was the epic crossing of the Atlantic Ocean, when, on November 10, 1940, it was used to inaugurate

The Atlantic Ferry Organization. Seven Hudsons, which were to fly in a formation led by Don Bennett (who later headed the Pathfinders of Bomber Command), took off from Gander, Newfoundland. Miraculously, after encountering a storm during which the aircraft were separated and were subjected to severe icing, all seven aircraft landed safely at Aldergrove in Northern Ireland.

It was cold on guard duty, especially in the early hours of the morning. Occasionally we would try to light a fire, providing we could find some wood. Most of the time, all we could do to keep the blood circulating was to pace back and forth unless we were at the bomb storage pit. Here we were able to build a shelter using discarded bomb storage containers. Also there was Skipper, a German shepherd, whose body heat would help as he lay at my feet in one of our shelters. Skipper's master had gone overseas, where he was believed to have been killed in action. Skipper must have missed his master because whenever he heard Bob, his master's name, he would go half crazy. He became the security guards' mascot, showing no favouritism to anyone in particular. Every evening he would leave our barracks and stay with one of us when we were on guard duty. While we were in Dartmouth, he was officially promoted to Leading Aircraftsman 2.

Guard duty was dull, except when we were caught "off guard," as was Jack Smith, one of my colleagues. One night, when Jack was slashing some wood with his bayonet trying to start a fire, he heard a rustling behind him. He paid no attention: he thought it was the paper he was crushing to start the fire. Then he heard, "ORDERLY OFFICER." Momentarily, he stood dumfounded, then collected his wits, grabbed his rifle, jammed on his bayonet and stood at attention. He expected to be reprimanded, but instead the officer had a corporal bring him some split wood.

There were other incidents involving guard duty that added a bit of humour to our lives. After we had been on duty for about four weeks, we were agreeably surprised when a group of older men joined us. These men were to be permanent guards. Like us they had received some training but, unlike us, a few of them took their responsibilities very seriously. Recruits undertaking guard training were told that to examine the pass of a suspicious person, they should have him lay his pass on the ground and place a stone or his watch on it and then to back up so that the guard could safely pick up the pass. In order to follow this procedure, one of the permanent guards always kept one of his pockets filled with stones so that he could throw them to suspicious persons. We thought this was crazy; imagine going on duty with a pocket full of stones. We nicknamed him "The General." We felt that he may have been mentally handicapped. He also took his duties seriously, too seriously in our view. One night he stood on a spot less than four feet in diameter for four hours. Another time, he had three airman lined up beside the hanger until he was relieved from duty. And, if that wasn't enough to convince his superiors that he needed psychiatric help, on a third occasion, he stopped the duty runway truck driver to see his pass.

Our accommodation was not good. Nonetheless, there were few serious complaints. We, I think, realized that Canada had not been well prepared for war and thus were willing to accept conditions considerably inferior to what many of us had experienced at home. We knew our guard duty responsibilities would soon end when our aircrew training began. Still, there was limit to our acceptance of what was expected of us. Our barracks were very cold, especially on the second floor where our section slept. In fact, it was so cold we could not sleep properly. So after a couple of nights, we were moved down to the ground floor. However, this caused severe overcrowding. We were so close together that I could touch the bunk beside me while I was in bed.

The food was reasonably satisfactory, but the catering staff felt they could do better if we would each chip in five cents a day. Based on today's prices a nickel may, if you are lucky, cover the cost of a candy but then, it was enough to pay for a scoop of ice cream or a cookie. Our menu for eight days beginning on April 3 was as follows

| | *Breakfast* | *Lunch* | *Dinner* |
|---|---|---|---|
| *Wednesday* | Corn flakes, Pancakes | Fish, Prunes | Eggs, Rice pudding |
| *Thursday* | Sausage, Oatmeal, Porridge | Stew, Cream pie | Sausage, Prunes |
| *Friday* | Bacon, Oatmeal Porridge | Fish, Prunes | Cold beef, Jell-o |
| *Saturday* | Beans & bacon, Oatmeal Porridge | Roast Beef, Raisin Pie | Stew, Apricots |
| *Sunday* | Ham, Eggs, Shredded Wheat | Steak, Ice Cream | Cold beef, Lettuce, Fruit Salad |
| *Monday* | Pancakes, Oatmeal Porridge | Cold beef, Corn, Apple Pie | Macaroni, Hamburgers, Apple Pie |
| *Tuesday* | Bacon, Oatmeal Porridge | Ham, Apple Sauce, Bread Pudding | Cold beans, Canned Pears |
| *Wednesday* | Sausage, Corn flakes | Fish, Pumpkin Pie | Beans & Bacon, Jell-o |

Halifax residents were much closer to the war than residents of interior cities, such as Montreal and Toronto. Just before we arrived in Dartmouth, a freighter carrying ammunition caught fire in the Halifax harbour. Had the crew not been able to check the fire, possibly a large part of the city would have been devastated as it was by a ship explosion during World War 1. On January 14, 1941, there were reports of a submarine having been sunk within sight of the Nova Scotia shore and there was considerable excitement when two German prisoners of war escaped from a ship in the harbour. We were cautioned to be especially alert while on guard duty. Fortunately, the Germans were soon recaptured, one in Halifax and the other in Dartmouth. Not long afterwards for reasons unknown to me, we were ordered to carry gas masks at all times and were given a taste of gas warfare by being subjected to tear gas in a gas chamber with and without our masks on.

There was not much for us to do whenever we had time off. There were movies in Halifax that we would attend occasionally and dances to which we airmen and other armed force personnel were invited. I only attended one of them because, not having danced before, I lacked the courage to ask young ladies to dance with me. I was fortunate, however, that I had become a friend of Paul Mosher, whose parents lived in Halifax. I enjoyed visiting his home and the delicious and appetizing meals his mother prepared. Those of us who had cameras would pass time in our barracks by taking photographs of each other in various poses. I had just purchased a camera that I kept by me during the remainder of my service in the RCAF. The arrival of mail was always a welcome diversion. I was particularly pleased to receive a sleeveless sweater knitted by Miss Watt, one of my high school teachers. This sweater, like my camera, remained in my possession for the whole of the war and returned with me to Canada from overseas. We would also occasionally hitchhike or go for long walks. I had never seen the ocean until four of us decided it was time that we did. It was a six-mile walk but at last there was me, a prairie boy, watching large breakers as they crashed onto the shore. I had always wanted to see the ocean. Now, finally, I had and I was impressed.

Some of us experienced short illnesses, which, in my case and in the case of a few others, resulted in hospitalization. I am not sure that the medical staff knew what was wrong with me, but I experienced a lot of pain in my joints. After being placed in isolation, I soon began to feel better and, after a day or two, I was complaining about the meals and the service I received. Five days later I was discharged and happy to be in fresh air and to taste good food again.

Two friends and our favourite pin-up, Esquire's Petty Girl

# CHAPTER 2

## *Learning to Navigate, to Drop Bombs and to Operate Machine Guns*

We were overjoyed when on April 9, 1941 more trainees arrived to take over our guard duty responsibilities. No time was lost. On the following day we departed Halifax for the Initial Training School in Victoriaville, Quebec. It was a happy journey for us all. Several of my mates became inebriated but I did not mind their boisterous behavior. In fact, I was impressed by their singing.

At last we were going to begin training, which would help us when we finally began to work for our wings, either those of an observer or a pilot. We were taught Morse code, aircraft recognition, mathematics and the importance of sanitation in promoting good health. Also we were given some exercises on link trainers, presumably to give us some idea of what pilot training entailed. Not unexpected in the military, there was drilling instruction on the parade square which helped maintain our physical health, as there were no sports activities while we were in Victoriaville.

My mates on our way to Victoriaville

I was favourably impressed with Victoriaville. Although many of the residents were not fluent in English, they were friendly and went out of their way to make me feel welcome. My first acquaintances were two brothers in their early teens. I cannot recall how we met, but for some reason the boys took an interest in me. I saw them from time to time. They spoke some English, which helped a lot to cement our relationship. They must have been impressed with their new friend because it was not long before I was invited to their home. After I left Victoriaville, we corresponded with each other several times.

While I enjoyed the boys' company, I was more interested in meeting young ladies. On April 19, I went on a girl-hunting expedition and it was not long before I arranged a date with an attractive young lady about my age who fortunately could speak some English. However, I almost messed up my first date with her. I called at the address she gave me and was invited in by a lady I assumed was her mother. I tried to make conversation but was not successful because she could not speak English and my high school French was not adequate. I could not understand why my date did not put in an appearance. Eventually, after what seemed a long time but probably was only twenty minutes, and after the lady had offered me a cup of tea, I realized she thought I had come to see her husband, who had not yet arrived home from work. I still don't know how I managed with a few words of fractured French and sign language to tell her that I had come to see her daughter. But, she indicated, she did not have a daughter. Suddenly her face brightened and she pointed up. She took me to her doorway and pointed to a doorway on the second floor, which was reached by exterior stairs. Sure enough when I rang the doorbell, it was opened by my date. I explained as best I could why I was thirty minutes late. She was very understanding. In the next few weeks, I enjoyed this young lady's company on several occasions at her home and in town. On one occasion, her parents took us for a drive in the country. On another occasion, I had to break off a date because I was confined to barracks for two days for being late for parade. (I had thought the parade was at ten-thirty a.m. rather than ten a.m. This proved to be the only time I was called on the carpet during my nearly five years in uniform.)

Maybe my problem was my big head. Here we were, experiencing warm spring weather, and I still had not received my service cap. Wearing winter headgear was most uncomfortable and made me the butt of jokes. I also had a problem with my feet. Presumably because of all the drilling we did, I wore large holes in the soles of my boots. Having only one pair, probably because I had such big feet, I had to wait in the shoe repair shop while they were being repaired. The shoemaker, an interesting person, spoke English reasonably well, so I did not mind waiting.

We did get two short leave periods. During our first leave, which was only thirty-six hours, a number of us, through the good fortune of being able to share a car, spent some time in Sherbrooke and Richmond. While I was impressed with the countryside, I did not enjoy the dance we attended in Sherbrooke because, as I have already noted, I could not dance. Fortunately, I did eventually learn to dance and attended many dances during my air force career. But more about that later. While in Richmond, we learned one of our fellow trainees had had his jaw broken in a fight. On my next leave, which I spent in Montreal visiting an aunt and her family, I paid a visit to our unfortunate comrade in hospital. He was making a satisfactory recovery. I never saw him again but I was pleased to note in the *Ottawa Citizen* many years later that he had survived the war and had been elected to a senior position in the Royal Canadian Legion.

On May 14, my birthday, our group began to be dispersed to various locations for more advanced training. I was pleased that we were finally going to be given some serious training. Nonetheless, I was sorry to see my new friends leave. By May 17, after all but six of my group had been posted, we learned we were to report to Manning Poole in Toronto. My spirits were high, as it had been rumoured that on our arrival we would be given seven days' leave. We were not disappointed. By late evening, May 21, I started hitchhiking to Bobcaygeon, arriving at my parents' farm at one a.m. My parents were surprised because I had not told them of my visit. It was a great homecoming. I visited many of my former schoolmates and all three of my teachers, who were pleased to see me. Even though I did not have a driver's license, my father let me have his Model A Ford for part of my leave. When he and one of the neighbours needed it to look for work, the neighbour let me use his car.

Time went quickly and on May 28, at one p.m. I was back on the highway just outside of Bobcaygeon with my right thumb in the air. I was lucky; I had no problems getting rides and by four-thirty I was in Manning Poole.

During the next few days we stayed in Manning Poole before we boarded the CPR train that was to take us to Prince Albert, Saskatchewan, where we would begin air navigation training. However, we did very little in the meantime that would help us achieve our goal–of becoming aircrew members. Most of our time was spent drilling and route marching–we were being used to promote the sale of war bonds. One Saturday as we marched along the streets of Toronto, I was impressed by the huge crowds lined up on the sidewalks, larger than I had seen when I visited Toronto on my bike to see the king and queen during their visit in 1939.

Feeding all of us was a major task for the air force. Consequently, it was not surprising when officers used us to perform onerous tasks in the kitchen. Whenever we missed a parade or drill practice, we were put on fatigue duty. This happened regularly as we did not always receive proper notice. I think this was deliberate policy as there were always bags of potatoes to be peeled. What better way to get the peeling done than by placing airmen on fatigue duty because they had missed a parade notice?

Our train departed Toronto about eleven-thirty p.m. on June 6. We arrived in Prince Albert about forty-six hours later at nine a.m. This included a stopover of five hours in Regina. Fortunately, for the first time since enlisting, we were given berths. This was not my first train journey across northern Ontario, Manitoba and part of Saskatchewan. Four years previously, in 1937, my father, my two brothers and I made a similar journey, but in two railway boxcars going in the opposite direction. That year my parents had made a courageous decision to leave their dried-out and grasshopper-infested farm in the southwestern part of Saskatchewan to seek greener fields in Ontario.

We were only at the Prince Albert air force base a few hours when our studies began. We were given aerial maps and then a lecture by the medical officer. I don't recall the contents of the lecture, but I assume safe sex was the main topic. During my introduction to life in the air force, I was warned on several occasions of the hazard of having sexual intercourse, particularly unprotected sex. While I was at Prince Albert, one my classmates apparently did not heed the advice because he was hospitalized with a sexually transmitted disease and taken off our course.

Life was not too bad at Prince Albert

We actually had little time for temptation. Our studies and flying instruction kept us busy during the days and into the evenings. Initially, I found the course difficult, but as time went by I began to do better. We soon realized that there were some risks attached to our training. During our course several aircraft crashed. Fortunately, there were no serious injuries. However, there were other problems. During warm weather the interiors of the Anson aircraft in which we trained became very hot and there was a disagreeable odour that seemed to be more pronounced at high temperatures. In addition, during flight, the bumpy movements of the aircraft caused by air drafts added to our feeling of discomfort. Consequently, it was not surprising that some of us became ill while in the aircraft. I often would feel like vomiting but, except for one occasion, I managed to keep my stomach under control.

At last, on Saturday, June 21, twelve days after our training had begun, I was able to visit Prince Albert and a day later three of us hitchhiked to Emma Lake in Waskesiu National Park. We had a great time, renting a boat with an outboard motor and later meeting two pleasant and attractive young ladies. None of us had ever been in a boat with a motor; I was put in charge. After I managed to get the motor started we began to explore the lake. Unfortunately, probably because I did not know the lake, I hit a rock, damaging the propeller. Having been brought up on a farm and being accustomed to working with machinery, I somehow managed with just my pocket knife to remove the propeller and replace the severed pin.

It would take two more months, July and August, before we completed the Air Observer Navigation course–two months of study and flying exercises with little time for recreation. We did get a few weekends off but, for the most part, we were on the go eight to ten hours a day and sometimes longer, as a few of us had to put in extra hours studying. I know I did. Exams were held from time to time and by the end of the course we had written eight. I passed, but not as well as I would have liked. I am certain some of my mates did considerably better. According to the certificate issued to me at the end of the course, I attained an average of 72.8%, enough to allow me to move on to the next courses–bombing and gunnery. I now had seventy-three hours of flying time of which eleven hours were night flying.

My mates at Prince Albert

Of course, we did occasionally have some time off base. Unfortunately, some of my mates, when enjoying their freedom from their studies and air force discipline, would consume more alcohol than they should have, which resulted in some rowdiness. Occasionally the rowdiness would become physical. Normally there were not any serious injuries–just a few bruises and maybe a black eye or two; but in one instance, a member of my class accidentally struck a young lady, knocking her unconscious. At other times, some would return late and would then find themselves restricted to base for seven and sometimes as many as fourteen days. For my part, if there was time, I with one or two others would hitchhike or catch a bus to Waskesiu National Park. I had enjoyed my first visit there and continued to enjoy subsequent visits. On our arrival on one of our visits to the park, we could not find any accommodation. Luckily, we met some young people who, learning of our predicament, took us to meet their parents who were spending the weekend at their cabin retreat. We were welcomed and stayed with them overnight.

While at Prince Albert, I had hoped to visit Mendham, which had been our hometown prior to my parents' decision in 1937 to pull up stakes for greener fields in Ontario. Through the co-operation of the administration staff and our senior instructor, arrangements were made for me to fly to Regina from where I was to find my way to Mendham. Unfortunately, an outbreak of sleeping sickness took place in Regina, resulting in my being recalled to Prince Albert. Eventually, after the war, I was able to visit what was left of our farm. The house was gone and the barn was leaning over but the trees that we–my father, my older brother and I–had planted had grown to a respectable height. They are probably are still growing. I hope so.

August 30 was an exciting day for us. We had completed our air observer course. Our next posting was to the Macdonald airfield near the tiny village of the same name north of Portage La Prairie, Manitoba. A large crowd came to the Prince Albert station to wish us well. I had not realized that we had made such a favourable impression on so many of the residents of the city. It made me feel good. At Macdonald, we received gunnery and bombing instruction qualifying us to bomb, fire machine guns and operate wireless equipment. Training was not nearly as onerous as it had been at Prince Albert. We enjoyed dances and vaudeville shows, which took place weekly. Also I had grandparents in Neepawa and an aunt and her family in Minnedosa whom I could visit.

Our gunnery and bombing training in the air was done in Fairey Battle aircraft, a combat single-engine aircraft that carried a crew of three. Its first flight was made in 1936 and at that time it was considered one of Britain's most advanced aircraft. However, early in the war its performance proved disappointing. Losses were very high and it soon was withdrawn from front line units to be used in training units. Nonetheless, to those of us who had never been in combat aircraft, it was exciting. Occasionally to show us what it could do and perhaps to relieve his boredom, our pilot would put it through a loop and slow rolls. What a change from the slow-moving Anson, which always was flown straight and level to help us develop navigational skills.

The author and a Fairey Battle aircraft, Macdonald, Manitoba

Saturday, October 11, was another exciting day for us. On parade we were presented with observer wings, which we proudly wore. There was not a large crowd to congratulate us; after all most of us were a long way from home. Still it was an important day for us. After months of study we at last had something to show for our efforts even though it was only half a wing. Nonetheless, it was special. As the war progressed navigation training was shortened. No longer were navigators required to know how to aim a bombsight, fire a machine gun or operate wireless equipment. On completion of their training those who had qualified were presented with wings not unlike the pilot wings. They were not as distinctive as the observer wing. Although we now had our wings, our training was not over. We still had to learn how to navigate with the stars. We would do that at Rivers, Manitoba, which was to be our home for the next four weeks.

Two days after our arrival at Rivers, a letter from home told me that Dad had given up farming. All our stock and farm equipment had been sold and Dad was following Mother to Toronto where he would be employed by General Electric. Mother had left some time before and now was working for G.H. Hees & Son, where she had worked during World War I when she met Dad. He had been a pilot with the Royal Flying Corps. Life on farms in Saskatchewan and

Ontario during the Depression years had been difficult. Now they thought with their three sons away–two in the air force and one as an apprentice to a plumber–they could turn over another leaf and try a new life in the city. Time would prove they made the right decision. I, however, would miss Rover, our dog, and Queenie, our pony, who had carried me over many miles in Saskatchewan.

Training exercises were not as difficult as at Prince Albert. At least, not for me. For the most part I did reasonably well, although flying in Ansons at between 8,000 to 10,000 feet in temperatures below 10° C was not a good working environment.

While in Rivers we did get some time off from our studies which I used to visit my aunt and her family in Minnedosa about eighteen miles northeast of Rivers. However, hitchhiking from Rivers could not always be counted upon to get me to my destination. After having to walk nine miles one Friday evening, I found myself marooned in Rapid City, which could have been more appropriately named Rapid Hamlet. Fortunately there was a small hotel, but that did not solve my problem. I had no money; I had left my wallet at camp. So I had to sleep in a chair in the lobby of the hotel. First thing in the morning as soon as there were signs of traffic, I took to the road again and arrived at my aunt's home in time for breakfast.

At Rivers there were few, if any, complaints about our accommodation and meals. However, I did come close to losing my temper one day. To enable us to get new clothing from time to time, a stores parade was held. We were required to line up alphabetically to wait our turn. The queue moved slowly. After three hours, just as I arrived at the wicket, it was shut without an apology. Of course I was not the only angry person, but I happened to be next in line. In the air force, patience was a virtue, which all of us did not have. Although, as time went on, we realized that waiting in line was a problem we would have to learn to accept.

# CHAPTER 3

## *Training Completed, We Depart for England*

On November 11, 1941, at five a.m. we began our train journey to Toronto to start a new phase in our air force career. We assumed our training was over and we would soon be flying on operations. Little did we know at the time that there was still more training ahead. I learned many years later when I received copies of my air force records that I had been recommended for a commission along with one other member of our class. For reasons unknown to me I did not receive that commission until March 1943. Perhaps it was for the best. Being a non-commissioned officer was not the end of the world. Possibly, at twenty years of age, I was not ready to assume the responsibilities of an officer.

While waiting in Winnipeg for the Toronto train, we had the misfortune of meeting a young lady who, while we were at Prince Albert, apparently liked to hang out with us. I don't know how she survived; I think she was a street person. While I can remember her as being reasonably attractive, we nonetheless soon tired of her company. However, we did not have the courage to tell her to get lost, so she was stayed with us for the whole day. I wonder about her occasionally. What happened to her? Did she meet other airmen? Was she able to turn her life around and become a useful member of society?

The train journey was boring; at least I found it so. I know I would find the journey more interesting today after living and working in Northern Ontario and Manitoba, and seeing first-hand the joys and hardships of the people who make their lives there. Upon my arrival, it took some time to locate my parents. They were not living together at the time. Mother had rented a room in a boarding house and Dad, before accepting employment with General Electric, was staying with a cousin in Woodbridge. Frank, my younger brother, was also there and would eventually become a plumbing apprentice to my dad's cousin. Eventually, I found my way to Woodbridge and later visited Mother at the George H. Hees factory. The next few days were spent visiting relatives and places of interest such as the Toronto Zoo, the Art Gallery and the Casino, Toronto's strip club. The gallery disappointed me. I don't recall why. Perhaps it was not surprising as I find myself still critical, perhaps overly so of the art on display in galleries. I guess I was not impressed with the Casino either as it is the only strip establishment I have ever visited.

Deciding to get out of Toronto for a few days, I put up my trusty thumb for a ride to Bobcaygeon. Since my parents had left the farm, my ties to my old home had changed, but it still turned out to be a special visit. I called on our former neighbours and hugged our old dog, Rover, whom my parents had to leave behind. The principal of the Continuation School was pleased to see me and encouraged me to write him from overseas. I did and welcomed his replies. It was gratifying to know he was interested in my welfare. Later he purchased a subscription to *Reader's Digest* for me, which, although I received it only sporadically, helped me cope.

On November 24, in the early afternoon, with my parents and high school friend Sheila waving goodbye, I boarded the train for Halifax. It was a difficult farewell. Would my parents and I see each other again? Would I see Sheila again, the girl with whom I used to walk to the high school? Although we had not seen much of each other after I had enlisted, I thought, as I said goodbye that perhaps fate would bring us together again if I survived the war.

On the train I was happy to meet a fellow airman who had been in my course at Rivers, but he was no longer an airman; he was a pilot officer. As far I was able to determine, he was the only member of our course to be promoted. The rest of us continued to wear sergeant strips for a long time.

Back in Halifax, we found better food and enjoyed better living accommodations. Since we had completed our training there was not much our superiors could find to occupy us while we were on standby waiting for transportation to England. Not surprisingly, route marches seemed to be their favourite way of keeping us active. Of course we also attended lectures on subjects that I have long since forgotten. We also had more free time than we had ever experienced previously. Fortunately for me, Paul Mosher[1] had also

[1] I learned years later that Paul was killed in action on July 10, 1942. The Whitley aircraft in which he and his fellow crewmembers were flying failed to return from operations.

completed his training and had joined us. As during our previous guard duty experience, he and his parents opened their home to us on several occasions. These visits helped relieve the boredom we were experiencing. As before, the meals prepared for us by Paul's mother were appreciated. I wondered if Mrs. Mosher noticed my new uniform, which had been issued to me soon after my arrival in Halifax.

Finally, on December 9, 1941, twelve months and three days after I had joined the RCAF, we embarked on a troop ship called the California. My feelings at the time of our departure can be gathered from the following excerpt taken from a notebook in which, from time to time, I expressed thoughts I could not express in my diary because of lack of space.

*Guns are booming, bombs are dropping, men are dying, women are weeping, children are crying. This is war, this is life; history is in the making. We are killing and being killed for a new order. War reminds me of blizzard in the West [of Canada]. I remember how comfortable and satisfied I felt when I was sitting in a house beside a fire with the wind wailing outside. Canada is just like that house: The oceans are its walls, the war in Europe is the blizzard and food and luxuries we have make up the fire. Most of us are thankful that we are sheltered from this war, but there are others who, not even satisfied with this, let their greed compel their minds to seek new ways and means to gain wealth from the blood we are spilling. We, on returning perhaps crippled and maimed for life, will use every drop of our weakened blood to make this new order, one that will be worth all this suffering and strife. Our sons will not say that we did not finish the job. They will not spend their youth in the shedding of blood. Their lives will be spent in making the world a better place in which to live.*

According to my notes, the California obviously disappointed me. Perhaps it is because I had expected more:

*From the rumours going around we were quite certain to have a cabin but most of us were given a berth. We had tea at 4:30 pm. That too disappointed me. All I had was a cup of tea, a piece of bread with a little syrup. We were not given any butter. The mess man said the amount of butter set aside for tea had already been used. It made me angry to think of all the cows I had milked and I could not even have one tiny speck of butter.*

*We are off [December 10]. We have been going for a few minutes now. I can feel the throb of the engines below me and the very slight sway of the ship. I had not thought last night that we would leave so soon. Most of us had gone to bed thinking we would get a good night's rest but that was not to be. Instead we almost froze to death. We are quartered in what I believe was a dining room. We could not be packed in more closely. The bunks are placed in tiers of three with about eighteen inches between each tier. I suppose we will all be sick. The ship's sway is more noticeable now. I am hoping I will get over it quickly.*

*This morning [December 11] we were told we would have the privilege of watching and hearing the ship's guns in action. I was so anxious to be on deck that I missed my dinner [lunch]. When the first gun went off, I believe I nearly passed away, the noise was so loud. The marksmanship seemed to be fairly accurate. The target may have been over or undershot slightly.*

*We have had another day at sea. All the anti-aircraft guns were fired. They were interesting to watch especially when you may be on the receiving end some day. The sea was quite rough. At least I thought it was but one of the sailors told me he had thought it would be much rougher. I don't think I am exaggerating when I say some the waves were twenty-five feet high. It is night now and the ship continues to plow through the sea. Today I had fancied the sea was raging thinking that it could not sink us. On leaving Canada the waves seemed to be whispering among themselves as if they held a secret. Perhaps they did but now they are angered and disappointed thinking that we may escape their cruel clutches as other ships have done.*

*We are on high seas now; at least it seems that way to me. I can hardly write because of the swaying, pitching and plunging of the ship. I was watching one of the two destroyers this afternoon that are accompanying us. One moment the sea would lift her boldly into view; at the next glimpse, all but her mast and the top of her funnel would disappear. On our ship it was like riding a roller coaster at Sunnyside [in Toronto]. First we would go up and the engines released from some of the water's pressure could be felt racing and throbbing from the very heart of the ship and then, I would feel an empty space in my stomach as the waves dropped us down gently but swiftly. Some of the sailors say they have not seen the sea much rougher but others tell us they saw it much worse. We don't know whom to believe. Perhaps some may have been pulling our legs.*

It was at this time that, struggling to steady my hand, I wrote "A Wave Speaks":

I am an Atlantic wave. I am strong. I show no mercy and ask for none in return. To me might is right. I wait and when an opportunity arrives, I strike; I show no remorse when I see these helpless humans struggling in my midst. Instead I laugh, for revenge to me is sweet. Ever since we were conquered by man, my comrades and I have patiently waited. Now when our foes are waged in controversy, our chance has come. All we do now is lie and wait, our cruel grasping hands ready to clutch and strangle those who come within our reach.

# CHAPTER 4

## *Introduction to England and the Royal Air Force*

*On climbing on deck on Thursday morning [nine days after we had left Halifax] all I saw was fog but then I took a closer look and I could see the faint outlines of many ships. We had anchored in some harbour during the night, which we later learned was Greenock near Glasgow. After waiting on deck for what seemed a very long time, we were given orders to disembark into a waiting ferryboat. As we stole inward through the fog, the first sign of war was a grounded blimp resting on shore. Shortly afterwards, looking upward, we saw two more blimps floating in the air tethered to the earth only by two slender cables attached to a small boat. Leaving the ferryboat, we climbed on board a train. I had seen photographs of British trains but had never thought of them as being so small. They are comfortable and fast but yet they are so different from our trains that we could not help making some rather rude remarks about them. The engines are so small and the boxcars are still smaller compared to ours. But enough of trains; we are moving at last.*

*I suppose we travelled over many of the picturesque areas of England, but soon the blackout compelled us to pull down the blinds and wait until morning before we could view the countryside. However, we did have time to see some bomb-wrecked homes and later several blimps high above us. The train rolled on, its wheels clicking on the rails, seeming to say ...-, ...-, V for Victory, V for Victory. . . .*

Ultimately, after twenty hours on the train, we arrived in Bournemouth on the south coast of England. That evening we experienced our first city blackout. We eventually became accustomed to them although we marvelled at how car drivers could find their way with headlights blacked out, except for a small hole about the size of a quarter. To welcome all the Canadians who had recently arrived in Bournemouth, the YMCA arranged a party. There was a lot of singing and some dancing. Unfortunately, I still did not know how to dance so could not muster enough courage to ask one of the many young ladies present to dance with me. Actually, I was hoping one of them would ask me, but it was not to be, so I returned to our residence feeling a bit melancholy. I need not have felt left out because the following evening there was another dance and, happily for me, an attractive WREN asked me to dance. It was wonderful and it was not long before I had no hesitation in asking girls to dance. I was no Fred Astaire but the girls did not seem to mind.

Christmas Eve found us in private billets. No transportation was provided so we, with our gear on our backs, walked the four miles to our new temporary home. By five I was settled and looking for something to do. I did not want to be alone on Christmas Eve. However, as I wrote in my notes, I was not alone for very long:

*I had no plans made for the evening when I overheard two fellow boarders say that they were going to a local pub. I suggested that I would like to accompany them. They consented and as a consequence I had my second beer in my life in the pub just a few blocks away. Soon our Canadian badges were noticed; people began to offer us drinks. Before I knew it I had four glasses of the rotten stuff. [I don't feel that way about beer now. In fact it did not take me long to begin to like it.] The smoke was stifling; you could hardly see through the haze. Across by the other bar, soldiers and their girls were showing their Christmas spirit by singing uproariously. I knew if I drank any more of the stuff, I would begin to feel its effect so I made some excuse and left. I grabbed a trolley to take me to Boscombe where I found soldiers and girls singing on the street and occasionally drunken laughter would break out. I was hungry, but the only cafes open were jammed to their doors. I arrived at our billet around twelve rather dejected because I really did not have a good time.*

That was my first Christmas Eve in England. My first Christmas Day, as recorded in my notes, was interesting and went a long way to boasting my morale:

*Christmas Day, an invitation to a private home, miles away and no bus service. How would we get there? Hitchhike of course and hitch we did. An army truck stopped in front of us. "Going our way buddy? Sure Canada, hop in." In we climbed and soon we found ourselves at our destination. That was service, that was the England I had dreamed of. Never let anyone down. The door was opened by a tiny greyhaired lady. Seeing who it was, she soon made us feel at home, keeping up a lively conversation all the while. She introduced us to her daughter, who was much like her. I knew we were in for a quiet afternoon. I decided to make the best of it and we soon had our hostess telling us of bombing raids. Apparently, England was not at all prepared for war. German reconnaissance planes flew over hours at a time stunting and looping, seemingly never disturbed by the RAF. The air force was hard put to guard ammunition dumps and manufacturing centres. Then the raids began; enemy aircraft flew so low that the pilot and his crew would easily be seen. Our hostess and her daughter had bullets striking the ground around them in their garden. On one occasion our hostess, out for a walk, heard a thump; she looked behind her and saw a German airman–dead because his parachute had not opened. These and other accounts she told us in an unconcerned manner as if they had been everyday occurrences.*

*We learned that some French soldiers from Dunkirk had landed on the coast near Bournemouth. "What a dejected lot they were," she said. "Some had no uniforms, others had incomplete uniforms; their socks clung to their skins and their bodies were covered with vermin." They too had not been ready when war was declared but it was these men who gave England time enough to wake up to the fact that a war was on. We owe a lot to these men who so gallantly but vainly attempted to hold France.*

Besides listening to our hostess's experiences of living in a country at war, we played Snakes and Ladders, hardly a game to excite airmen and put us in a Christmas mood. Not surprisingly, as soon as we felt we could leave without offending our hostess, we did. The party at the YMCA beckoned us and helped us to enjoy our first Christmas outside of Canada.

For the next few days all we were required to do was to take part in a few parades. We were being kept in Bournemouth until a training establishment could take us. I had thought that I had completed all the training required to enable me to join a squadron. Not so. There were still months of training ahead of us. According to circulating rumours, we were to receive a short leave followed by a posting to a training unit. They proved true. On December 30, I was given five days' leave. Fortunately I did have some relatives in England and I decided to visit a great aunt at Prestbury near Cheltenham. I managed to get a message to her, but I don't remember how. Her home address, Frogmore Villa, intrigued me because it was my understanding that only the very rich or prominent people gave names to their homes. Would she have a doorman and other servants?

The train journey was tiresome. In my diary I went so far as to call it *wretched*. Unfortunately, I missed a connection with the consequence I did not arrive in Cheltenham until three a.m. Finding a place to bed down for the remainder of the night was not easy; finally, I did get one at the YMCA. All turned out well. By nine-thirty that morning I was ringing the bell of Frogmore Villa. It proved to be an attractive home, but nothing like I envisaged. There was no doorman to greet me but my aunt more than made up for his absence. There were other relatives to welcome me–my aunt's son, his wife, and their twelve-year old son John, who would become my pal during this and subsequent visits. It was not an exciting stay but an enjoyable one. On New Year's Day I was taken to visit distant relatives nearby who were farmers. This was particularly enjoyable because, having been brought up on farms in Saskatchewan and Ontario, I was intrigued by farming in England. Of course I found my aunt's home interesting as well. First I had trouble adjusting to the low temperature of the house. The only warm area was directly in front of the fireplace. The kitchen was not as well equipped as Canadian kitchens, either. There were few cupboards and the gas stove was small. Hot water, when available, was supplied by a water heater in the bathroom. Because of wartime fuel rationing, the heater was only turned on when required and then not long enough for a pleasant bath. Anyway the bathroom was so cold that baths were naturally cut short. However, it was in my Aunt Bessy's home that was I introduced to tea brought into my bedroom in the morning while I was still in bed. I never did become used to this custom and can't say I appreciated the tea. If you were not ready to get up before the arrival of the tea, you certainly were after you had drunk it.

On January 3, 1942, at eight p.m., I stepped down from the train in Bournemouth. The next evening, according to my notes,

My great-aunt Bessie and family

*I am sitting in Betty's Cafe ready to partake of what I hope will be fish and chips, not just chips. My thoughts go back to a movie I saw this afternoon. I thought of myself enjoying a movie while other men are living just to die. They know they have not a chance but their loyalty for their country compels them to fight until they can fight no more. I know that aircraft would help but here I am, a trained observer, grumbling about a mere meal while those men are crying for help from the air.*

Shortly after my return, other Canadian airmen and I were told to prepare to depart for Millom, Cumberland, in the north of England not far from the Lake District, a favourite tourist destination in peacetime. But it wasn't until five p.m. on January 5 after one train cancellation that we boarded a train that eventually would take us there. I say eventually because having to be routed through London, we did not arrive at Millom until eight-thirty the following morning. On our journey we tried to have some WAAF members join us in our section but were not successful. They must have been forewarned against fraternizing with a virile group of Canadian airmen.

Our introduction to life with the RAF was not exactly a bed of roses. We were quartered in Nissen huts, about twenty airmen to a hut with our cots lined up on each side with a small coal-fired heater in the centre for which we never had enough coal. There was not a warm location in the whole camp for us sergeants. We did not even have a canteen. As noted below, the only time we really felt warm was when we had a bath.

*On being sent to a RAF training establishment, I had expected to find everything done efficiently and effectively. In this I was disappointed. Just as in Canada, we often are kept waiting, doing nothing. But that is not all; planes are sent up unserviceable. One was not completely fueled, another had a faulty engine and one landed with a flat tire. Sometime every night since we have been flying something seriously happens to one of our aircraft. A plane crashed in the Irish Sea near here. The crew is lost. Jamie's plane caught on fire last night. He managed to put it out but his map was burned. We fly tonight [January 11]. Did not fly last night. Plane unserviceable. Observed my first German air raid. Saw anti-aircraft fire. Our A/C could not land but had to circle the aerodrome. Many A/C lost. All accounted for later. One crash landing.*

*January 13. "Wakey! Wakey!" seemed to come to me in a dream. I curse under my breath. Was it morning already? I roll over and then begin to appreciate the warmth of my cot. I doze off only to be rudely wakened again by a tug on my blankets. "Get up Pat, it's seven-thirty and you're supposed to be flying this morning." Aw hell, I had forgotten. Nothing for it but to get up. Pushing my head above the blankets, I see my breath and feel the damp cold on my shoulders. There were only two other boys getting up; the others are sleeping as if it were the middle of the night. I crawl out of bed but when the cold takes effect, I soon am scrambling into my clothes. Three minutes later I am washing in the cold unheated washroom. Fortunately for us, the water is always warm. By eight I am in the mess partaking of our scanty breakfast, porridge without milk or sugar, tea that tastes of soap and noxious tasting pork. This was the beginning of a new day in the RAF. Nothing to write about. What do you think?*

For the most part life at Millom was boring if you discount the problems we encountered when flying in often poorly maintained aircraft. What to do for entertainment and relaxation? Attend movies, go for long walks, play snooker, join the locals in the Millom hotel pub or visit Barrow, the closest city, to enjoy a change in food. Occasionally, a dance was held in camp where we would have an opportunity to dance with Women of the Auxiliary Forces (WAAFs) and some of the local young ladies. There were not many of them, so dancing opportunities were limited. I don't recall anyone becoming involved with any of the girls. They knew and we knew that the Millom air base would not be our home for long. We enjoyed the train rides to and from Barrow, possibly because the way some of the coaches were divided into separate sections so that they could be entered only from the outside of the train. Thus, as is normal for young people, we could be noisy without disturbing other passengers. Some coaches were first class. As sergeants we were expected to travel second class but when the coaches were overly crowded, we would occasionally occupy the more comfortable coaches.

As already noted, not only was the food poor, it was also poorly prepared. One day the fish we were served for dinner had not been properly cleaned. Imagine finding a fish hook in a fillet of fish served to you as one of my friends did. Our welfare officer was bombarded with complaints, all to no avail, until three weeks after the fish complaint, we learned that a high-ranking officer from headquarters would make an inspection.

*All permanent personnel paid a little more attention to their work today than they usually do. Two Canadian welfare officers and some high-ranking English officers, including an air-vice marshal, made an inspection of the camp. As would be expected the station was warned of this inspection a week before it was to take place. Consequently, everyone was on his toes and everything was being done to pull the wool over the inspecting officers' eyes. The officers here seem to have a knack for that sort of thing. The cups we were lacking in our mess appeared today; the meals were served on time and we could help ourselves. The change in the tea was remarkable. I think all our tea ration for next week must have been used today. In addition, we could add as much sugar and milk as we pleased.*

*One of the most striking instances of wool-pulling took place in the operations [ops] room. The class members there were not going to fly unless the inspecting officers arrived. The officers did come. You should have seen the change; the ops room became a real ops room; the weather conditions existing over the flight route and the target and dangers involved were fully explained and described; an explanation of the method of opening the bomb door was provided. But the operational instructions and information was not the only surprise. Instead of walking across the field to their aircraft, the boys were given a ride and found the aircraft warmed up with an officer to show them to their aircraft. They took off and circled the field until the inspecting officers had left the field, then landed. That was not all; obviously no [practice] bombing was planned, as there were no bombs in the aircraft. However, I think the camp officers were foiled in their attempt to deceive the inspecting officers. I believe some of our boys saw that the truth was revealed during the informal talk we had with the inspecting officers that evening.*

Although we were pleased that our meals did improve after the visit of the inspecting officers, life went on as usual. We continued to be bored a lot of the time because when flying was cancelled due to unfavourable weather our superiors had difficulty replacing our flying time with useful training activities. Instead, we played snooker in the Millom hotel and went to dances and movies in Millom and Barrie. In January and February, there was much more snow than I had expected in England. Fortunately, it usually melted quickly, but not always. As there was no snow removal equipment in camp, on a number of occasions we were ordered to clear the runways with shovels. A slow way to clear snow, but at least it was a way to keep us busy.

Weather conditions made flying hazardous and, on February 28, 1942, an aircraft was reported missing. I made a note of the tragedy on March 8:

*Visibility is nil. There is ice forming on the wings. The usually nervous pilot is becoming more nervous still. His mind is torn between the thought whether he should go up above five thousand feet and face the wrath of Fighter Command or take a chance of getting out of the freezing temperatures by reducing his altitude. He decides to go down. All the while, the two young Australian observers sit tight hoping that common sense will make the pilot try to get above the clouds. But they are hoping in vain. The plane goes down. They peer out but can't see any waves. The altimeter reads 500, 300, 150, 60 feet and then with a shudder the plane strikes water. The fuselage splits in half. Locked like rats in the wreckage, they think of their mothers and perhaps their sweethearts before they go down, never to come up, to taste the sweet folly of life again.*

*This may have been what occurred a week ago in freezing cloud over the wind-roughened sea. There was hope that only one of their engines may have failed. Perhaps they had time to get into their dinghy. It was because of that hope that our commanding officer decided to attempt a search and rescue mission the following day even though the weather had not improved. Experienced navigators were only chosen first. Twice we almost left the ground before flying was washed out. Organization of the rescue mission was poor; no one seemed to want to take on the responsibility of sending us up. We continued to hang around until early afternoon. All this time, those men if they were alive would be anxiously listening and scanning the heavy cloud above their wave-rocked dinghy. Our first navigator, thoroughly fed up with the way the search activity was being managed, left us. I took his place accompanied by a second pilot.*

*We took off but we were hardly airborne when we were ordered to return. It was not possible to land because the cloud was so low we could not see the runway. Our pilot had had enough; he asked for a course to Jurby on the Isle of Man, the nearest airport. There would be no search attempt as far as he was concerned. His decision was probably right under the circumstances but I felt otherwise. We were up; I could see no reason why we should not carry out the search. It seemed as if the pilot had forgotten those men whom we hoped were afloat on the cold windswept sea. They had risked their lives for the same reason we were risking ours so why should we not sacrifice our comparative safety to perhaps find them, thus stopping the flow of tears their mothers would shed for them?*

Perhaps I was overly critical of my pilot. After all, I was only an airman under training and knew very little about search and rescue operations.

There was no improvement in the weather. All flying was scrubbed for days. There was nothing to do except hang around the sergeants' mess at Jurby or visit Ramsay, a small town nearby. We had no change of clothes so you can imagine how we felt when finally, on the sixth day, the weather cleared and in less than an hour we were back on the Millom airfield. I was happy to see my buddies. Life went on–more training, more visits to Barrow and the billiard room in the Millom hotel, and more boredom. With spring the weather improved and we could relieve the boredom by playing softball and soccer. But one day when we were off duty, two of us had a better idea as to how to put in our time. We would rent bikes and tour the Lake District. Unlike the bikes available today, they were single speed, which meant we would have to walk up many of the hills in the district. Had we known what to expect perhaps we would not have started the cycle. The following description of the cycle is taken from a letter I wrote home on March 26, 1942.

*I spent last Saturday, a day off, cycling through the Lake District, a well-known resort area. The two of us certainly enjoyed the trip covering over sixty miles before we reached home. We departed at nine and arrived home just before the blackout. I was ready to drop. Except for the road along the shore of Lake Windermere, we were continually going up and down hill. We didn't think much about having to walk up them, but we more than made up for the time lost when we raced down, passing cars and frightening people. I did not have very efficient brakes and there were many times when I almost ran into brick walls. Frank [my brother], I know you would have enjoyed the trip. The scenery, as was the day, was perfect. Lake Windermere I imagine looks a lot like the lakes at Banff. We had gone 64 miles. The scenery was very beautiful. We saw the greater part of the Lake District, visiting Ambleside and Windermere. We were very tired when we got back.*

Cycle tour around Lake Windermere

Soon after we returned, a rumour that we would soon receive eight days' leave was circulating the camp. Finally the rumour became a reality and on March 30 I caught a train at the Millom station to take me north to Whitehaven. I was on my way to visit a family in Scotland at Muirkirk who, through a relative in Canada, had invited me to spend my leave with them. The train journey was slow. I spent the night in Whitehaven sleeping on the floor of the YMCA while waiting for a connection to Carlisle–not because I was short of money, but because there was no other accommodation available.

At last, I arrived at Muirkirk, a small town in the heart of a coal mining area. My host family was prominent in the Muirkirk community. The father, the manager of a coal mine, and his family lived in an attractive home which stood by itself at the end of a tree-lined lane. I was given a royal welcome by the family–the host and hostess and their two daughters, Christine and Sheila. I was impressed particularly with Christine, who was about my age. Perhaps if circumstances had been different, I would have fallen in love with her, but that was not to be. Three days after my arrival, I received a phone call ordering me to return to Millom. My posting to an operational training unit (OTU) had come through. I had had a wonderful time during those three days, during which I enjoyed a visit to Glasgow with Christine. In my diary I had this to say about her:

*This is first time I was with a girl who really tried her best to have me enjoy myself. I will be lucky if ever I meet as nice a girl again.*

On the third day the three of us, Christine, Sheila and I caught the train for Ayr where I had my first and only skate overseas. Although the ice was soft, I nonetheless had a great time with the sisters. Not surprisingly, my feelings on leaving Muirkirk were mixed. I would have liked to stay longer, but at the same time I was looking forward to leaving Millom. For some time I corresponded with Christine, but I did not realize that her parents expected her to read all her incoming letters to them. I unfortunately referred to remarks Christine had made about a young man with whom she was acquainted, remarks that she had no intention of revealing to her parents. As a consequence, Christine was reprimanded by her parents, and I felt perhaps it would be best that I discontinue my correspondence with her. Her parents would be certain to insist on hearing what I had to say.

# CHAPTER 5

## *Operational Training at Upper Heyford, Oxfordshire*

We departed Millom on April 6, 1942. Upper Heyford, a permanent RAF station a short distance north of Oxford, would be my new home for the following three months. Not unexpectedly, the train was crowded. For many of us, there was standing room only. On making our way along the corridors of the cars, we noted that in a first class section several seats were empty, and we took them although we did not have first class tickets. However, only officers traveled first class, as was pointed out to us to us very strongly by one of the three ladies seated in the compartment. In my letter home of April 9 soon after we arrived as Upper Heyford, I had this to say about this particular episode:

*For the greater part of the journey we traveled first class although we only had third class tickets. A haughty lady accompanied by two other ladies demanded that her compartment be cleared. "They are only sergeants," she observed. We did not budge; we did not appreciate her attitude. The conductor said nothing; he was an ex-serviceman. Consequently the lady and her friends stood in the aisle.*

If the ladies had stopped to think a minute, they would have realized we would be officers in as soon as six months–if we survived. Other than take the empty seats, we did not do anything to antagonize them, so they inconvenienced themselves for nothing.

Things were looking up. Spring had arrived and what a grand spring it was; the sun appeared almost every day and there was little rain. The summer, too, was great but somewhat cooler than the summers I had experienced in Canada. We found Upper Heyford much more agreeable than Millom. Oxford, an attractive and interesting city, was only a short bus ride away.

But there was little improvement in our meals. We continued to look forward to our food parcels, especially those that contained peanut butter and honey. Also with the coming of spring, we borrowed bikes to call on neighbouring farmers to purchase eggs from them.

Although we complained a lot about our meals, we really were not difficult to please as is revealed in a letter I wrote home on June 10.

*I have just finished a super supper of bacon and an egg with a cup of coffee. I supplied nothing this time. Happy got the bacon from a ration card he had not used on his leave, the egg from a local farmer and the coffee from a parcel.*

In another letter written earlier, I made the following comments on parcels.

*You will be surprised to know that no. nine parcel arrived before your letter by five days. I am enjoying the contents now. The chocolates Harold [my brother] sent me certainly were good. Don't send me any more cocoa. I have more than I will use in a long while. Sandwich spread does not go over very well because we get so many different kinds of prepared meats now. Jam, honey and peanut butter go over best. The cake was very good.*

Training went on much as it had at Millom, except there was more of it; and the training was done in Wellington aircraft rather than the Ansons in which I had done practically all my previous training both in Canada and at Millom. The Wellington, a two-engine bomber aircraft, was still being used on operations by a few squadrons. As at Millom there were crashes. In my diary I reported four in which seven airmen were killed. The cemetery nearby was full of white crosses of airmen who had been killed while on training exercises. My navigation training was uneventful until I was told on May 5 that I and a number of other navigators would now undertake the bomb-aiming course. The RAF needed more bomb-aimers. I was angry; I had always assumed I would fly as a navigator. Anyway, there was nothing I could do but carry on.

I continued to visit Oxford occasionally when we were given time off. As noted in my diary, dates with young ladies in Oxford were not always without mishap:

*Made a date [by phone] with a girl in Oxford. Turned out there were two girls with the same name working for the same employer. Made the date with the wrong one so waited in vain while the other girl waited on the other side of the street. Finally went to the dance and met the girl with whom I thought I had made the date. I had a good time.*

Residents of the city of Birmingham invited members of the Canadian armed forces to spend a weekend with them. Canadians at Upper Heyford were included. All we had to do was get to Leamington where we could catch buses that would eventually take us to the YMCA in Birmingham and our hosts. We departed Upper Heyford early on a Friday morning. Our interesting and enjoyable day had begun. Our first stop was Warwick Castle, whose history goes back to the 900s. We were impressed and it continues to impress the many tourists who visit it. Unfortunately, we could not tour the interior as it was being used to house government offices. We could, however, tour the grounds, after which we viewed a home built in 1383 by the Earl of Warwick for use as a retirement home by his servants. He and his servants had long since departed and were at the time of our visit replaced by members of the armed forces.

Horsing around

After an enjoyable and appetizing lunch provided by the people of Warwick, we boarded our buses to Stratford-on-Avon. There we toured the home in which Shakespeare was born and of the home of his wife, Anne Hathaway. The fact that these two homes were still habitable impressed me, a Canadian, who had never been in a home more than fifty years old. We, of course, could not leave Shakespeare's birthplace without a tour of the theatre erected to commemorate the great bard. As noted in the following excerpt from a letter to my parents, I was not overly impressed. Possibly now, if I were to visit Stratford, I would have a different opinion:

*We were told it is one of the finest examples of architecture in the world but to tell the truth, I could see nothing exceptional about it.*

Training continued. Almost every day I flew on training flights of about two hours' duration, improving my map-reading, gunnery and bomb-aiming skills. I believed I was making reasonable progress until one morning I woke up with a swelling on the side of my face. I had the mumps! Six o'clock that evening found me in the forces hospital at Halton. I stayed on my back for eleven days. Not surprisingly I felt miserable. Fortunately I was not alone. For a while I shared a room with Happy, who had been the first in our group struck down with mumps. Later when he left I shared the room with another mumps-stricken victim. In the meantime, there was little that I could do but write letters and read. My mail did get through occasionally, which was a great morale booster. To help put in the time and to amuse ourselves, the two of us, in bed facing each other, would toss coins at ashtrays on each other's bed. I also worried about falling behind in my training. I did not relish the thought of starting afresh with new crews.

The nursing sisters were a great help. They would drop in to talk to us whenever they had time. They even shortchanged Happy' s sheets the day before he was scheduled to return to Heyford. The following diary entry describes one of my more embarrassing incidents in the hospital.

*Had a dose of [Epsom] salts this morning. Received an urgent call of nature later. Dashed out, reached the toilet when it started. Poor me. Luckily there was an extra pair of pyjamas in the bathroom.*

Thirteen days after my admission to the hospital, I was back at Upper Heyford. I was given seven days' leave, which I did not want, as I was most concerned I would be left behind when my course was posted to squadron operations. Following a meeting with the adjutant, I was permitted to return to my course. Shortly afterwards, I learned that a friend, David Baird, a bomb-aimer like myself, had been reported missing from Bomber Command's first one-thousand bomber raid, which took place over Cologne. Arthur Harris, Chief of Bomber Command, realized that, although his command had had some recent successes, notably against Lübeck and Rostock in northern Germany east of Hamburg, the future of the command was not secure. He wanted some spectacular successes so he proposed that the command launch one thousand bomber raids. Unfortunately, there were not enough seasoned crewmembers and so some were drawn from training units. David Baird was one of those chosen. Possibly I would have been chosen as well, but perhaps fortunately for me, I had not yet been discharged from hospital. As David had been a fellow trainee from the very beginning of my aircrew training, it was difficult for me to accept his probable death. A Newfoundlander, he was the first of many friends and associates who would give their lives for their country.

According to my notes made some time later and to official records, David lost his life on May 31, 1942, at age twenty. While returning from Cologne after the first of the one thousand bomber raids, both engines of the Wellington bomber lost power over the North Sea and David bailed out as ordered. The engines suddenly regained power; possibly the higher temperature at the lower altitude had reduced the icing conditions that had adversely affected the delivery of gasoline to the engines. The pilot regained control and was able to bring the aircraft safely back to Heyford. All other members had not had time to bail out and thus survived to fly again. David has no known grave; his name is inscribed on the Runnymede War Memorial, at Surrey, England.

Although I was officially on leave, as permitted by the adjutant, I resumed my training and returned to Course 34. I had been worried that I would be put on a succeeding course and thus would have had to give up the many contacts and friendships I had already made. I was particularly concerned about crewing up. I wanted very much to be crewed up with aircrew I had gotten to know intimately. Fortunately (at least at the time I thought so) I was able to strike up a pleasant relationship with Pilot Officers Madson and Donovan, respectively from Winnipeg and Toronto. I had associated with them a few times on visits to local pubs and to Oxford where on one particular evening, we–even I who normally rationed my drinks–possibly drank more alcoholic beverages than we were capable of managing without showing signs of inebriation. I don't remember what happened to Donovan that night, but Madson and I missed the last bus to Upper Heyford with the consequence that we had a long walk ahead of us. Not long after returning, we–including Donovan, who somehow had found his way home–and the remainder of the crew were in the air on a training flight. I learned my lesson: no carousing the day before a flying exercise.

Life went on. We continued to bitch about our meals and to scrounge the countryside for eggs. We could usually buy a half-dozen from a kind farmer's wife. Eggs, just plain ordinary everyday eggs, did a lot to bolster our morale. At breakfast I would hand them into the kitchen and have them prepared, much to the chagrin of other airmen who had not been able to scrounge as successfully as I.

Cockroaches were a problem in the kitchen and dining hall. One evening at supper, an airman displayed cockroaches that he had just removed from a jar of jam. Nonetheless, we survived. We may have complained about the food, but I don't recall any long periods of hunger.

June 26, 1942 found me in one of our training aircraft, a Wellington bomber, headed for Bremen, Germany. We were one of the 1,067 aircraft that took part in this raid. While our target was the docks, I don't know where our bombs exploded, as the target area was covered by cloud. A bank of cloud was known to be in the area some hours before takeoff, but Bomber Command meteorologists had forecast that the cloud would be blown eastwards by a strong wind by the time of the raid. Not surprisingly, the results were not dramatic. Still, a Focke-Wulf aircraft factory, the shipyard and docks, and four important industrial factories were partially destroyed. My diary entry concerning this flight is as follows:

*Did go on an operations flight over Bremen. There was plenty of ack-ack but it did not look as deadly as it really is. We came home not knowing that we had three holes in one wing. On landing we had enough petrol to last a half hour. One of the aircraft from our OTU did not return.*

We resumed our training exercises. My training for the most part continued to focus on improving my machine-gun and bombing accuracy. I flew almost every day, sometimes twice a day. I did reasonably well. To hone our machine-gun skills, we were required to shoot at a drogue pulled on a long cable by another aircraft. One afternoon after shooting many rounds, I decided I had had enough, so I aimed at the cable where it joined the drogue. In a matter of minutes, we were returning to base. I had severed the cable, bringing the exercise to an abrupt end.

No further losses of airmen took place during this period of my training, but there were close calls. Because of poor visibility, two aircraft almost collided in mid-air. On two occasions I was told that I was slated to fly operationally, but fortunately perhaps for me, and the others who would fly with me, the flights never took place. Losses of OTU aircraft on the Thousand Bomber Raids were reported higher than those of Bomber Command squadrons. This was not surprising, since, except for the pilot, the crews were inexperienced. Also the Wellington aircraft in which many of the OTU crews flew were slower than the Lancaster and Halifax aircraft used by most of the command squadrons.

My course at Upper Heyford

# CHAPTER 6

## *Training Over, Life Begins on a Bomber Command Squadron*

At last we completed our training. It took the air force eighteen months to train me to fly on a bomber squadron. But first we were given seven days' leave. Six of us, all sergeants except for one officer, decided we would go to Windermere, in the Lake District. I don't remember who suggested it; perhaps it was I, because I had been impressed by the district during my bike ride in March.

Following a day's stopover in London where some of our group went on a pub crawl, we departed London at noon, arriving very hungry in Windermere at seven-thirty. The hotel management probably was somewhat surprised at our arrival because few servicemen would choose Windermere for a break. During the war it was a favourite resort for older people many of whom were retired.

Our accommodation, while adequate, was far from luxurious. We shared a long, narrow room on the top floor separate from the other rooms. I presume management was concerned that we would disturb other guests. They were right, because some of my colleagues spent more time in the pubs than they should have. It was during this leave that I discovered a boilermaker–a shot of hard liquor followed by a glass of beer. A few of these drinks were all I needed to put me on "Cloud Nine."

Although there were few other young people around, we did have a good time. We rented bikes on two occasions so as to see more of the area in and around Windermere. Unfortunately, McBurney, the officer, ran into a stone fence, severely bruising his forehead, which we covered with a bandage. Not surprisingly, the bike shop owner would no longer rent bikes to us, but that did not stop us from having a good time. First we tried to rent saddle horses, but without success. Possibly the stable owner had heard of our bicycle mishap, so was concerned about how we would manage on his horses. He was probably justified because my friends, considering all the alcohol they consumed, might have had difficulty mounting and staying on their steeds. Our only recourse was to rent boats, which we did–rowboats and sailboats.

We could handle the rowboats easy enough, but when it came to the sailboat, we had trouble. Only one of us had ever sailed before so it was not long before we ran aground some distance off shore. We had no choice but to get out of the boat. I could not swim, so I held on to the boat as the others tried to rock it loose. Two young ladies came on the scene in a rowboat to watch the stupid Canadians trying to re-float their sailboat. I climbed into their boat and left my friends to fend for themselves. Eventually they returned to shore none the worse for their experience.

On leave at Lake Windermere

The following account of our last evening in Windermere is taken from my notebook:

*For me the night is over; the streets are deserted; the boys are likely in a pub; there is nothing for me to do but to go back to the Stag's Head for the last time. I went through the doorway and had started up the stairs to our room when I heard sounds of gaiety from the smoke room. Perhaps the night was not over for me. I had to look and there in the corner surrounded by the boys was the pantry maid sitting up straight, singing lustily, a cigarette in one hand, a glass of beer beside the other. She sat there, a neat, tiny old lady, her hair tied behind her head, which she held slightly back as she sang with two sound front teeth showing and her right hand slowly tapping out the rhythm of old Irish tunes. She did not think she should stay with the guests, as she was only the pantry maid. She kept constantly getting up to go but MacKenzie would break in saying, "To hell with them, you're staying here." She did stay, singing song after song, smoking cigarette after cigarette, and drinking whisky, one shot after another. She held her own and was able to say goodbye to us, when we, feeling the effects of the evening, were ready to call it a day.*

In summary, our holiday was a success. We had fun even though the weather was partially overcast most of the time and there were few young ladies to attract us. There was one bonus. We met a British major, Reg Lecoustre, and his wife, who were always around and they seemed to help us enjoy life as we found it at Windermere. But perhaps best of all were the older guests of the Stag's Head Hotel. They understood our need to unwind before we faced searchlights and ack-ack over Germany. On the evening before our departure they were all in the smoke room to say goodbye. But we saw some of them again. As we checked out early in the morning, they were there once more to wish us Godspeed.

My destination was Syerston, a large and comfortable pre-war airfield where I was to serve on 61 Squadron, 5 Group, Bomber Command, which, at the time of my arrival, was in the process of converting from Manchester to Lancaster aircraft. The airfield was near the small village of Syerston in the Midlands on the Trent River about halfway between Nottingham and Newark. Like most squadrons in 5 Group, 61 Squadron consisted of two flights, each of which contained between eight and ten aircraft. Since each aircraft carried a crew of seven, well over 140 members of aircrew were required to keep the aircraft in the air while allowing time off for crewmembers. Besides aircrew there were the support staff, which included ground aircraft service crews, drivers, control tower personnel, medical staff and welfare personnel. My colleagues and I were fortunate that 61 Squadron was converting to the Lancaster aircraft, which, with its four engines, was a much better aircraft than its two-engine predecessor. That may well account for my being here today trying to write this account of my life with the RCAF.

Fortunately for me I found my pilot, Madson, and navigator, Donovan, at the Newark station waiting for a truck to take them the

A Lancaster aircraft

remaining few miles to our new home at Syerston. Sadly, it would not be Madson's home for very long. Shortly after we had settled in, the squadron was loaned to Coastal Command to undertake patrol activities. This transfer of the squadron's responsibilities was only for a short time, but long enough, unfortunately, for us to lose our pilot. To gain operational experience, Madson flew as a second pilot on sea patrol over the Bay of Biscay. The aircraft never returned. According to the official record of the flight, the crewmembers were killed in action. I learned the day after (May 21) that Madson, along with other members of the crew, had been reported missing. Here is what I wrote that day in my notebook:

*Today I learned that our pilot, Jack Madson, is reported missing. No word has been received from the aircraft after it took off. We can only guess at what happened: perhaps a Jerry fighter scored a lucky hit or they may have been hit by heavy flak from the ship they were sent out to destroy. [Actually, as already noted, they were sent on patrol and not necessarily to attack enemy ships.] Jack is my second close friend who has been reported missing. We have no definite proof that there is no hope. He may be safely on board as a prisoner of war on the very ship they tried to bomb or he may even be back in England after being rescued from their dinghy. But on the other hand if we face facts, there were not any messages sent from the aircraft and therefore they must have been caught off-guard or have been hit by a very lucky shot from an enemy ship.*

*Jack was a regular fellow. I have known him since the first week in April and in that time I learned to appreciate what a fine person he was. As a captain, he was tops. He would go out of his way to make things easier for his crew. He invited criticism and even expected it. He was a good pilot and was always trying to improve his flying. It is too bad that chaps like Jack must leave this world, but war takes all as they come and makes no choice between the good and the bad.*

My letters home and diary entries state that I found Syerston a great improvement over Millom and Upper Heyford. In a letter dated August 8, 1942, I described my room, which I shared with Ralph Woolley, whom Madson had chosen as our wireless operator.

*I am writing this letter from our cozy room in our mess. It leaves nothing to be desired. We have a neat desk and large lockers. We also have two chairs, one of which is a comfortable armchair. The room is steam-heated, so we should be comfortable in the winter. All rooms have one large window that opens outward. If we wish we can hang pictures on the walls. Our cots are quite comfortable.*

Although the meals served in the sergeants' mess were much better than I had experienced at the other stations, we would periodically cycle into the countryside to visit local pubs and cafes for variety. I managed to acquire a bike from the transport section of our station. It was a woman's bike, which irked me a bit but, nonetheless, I was happy to have it. Sometime later I purchased a man's bike from an airman and I used it for the remainder of my career in Bomber Command. On one of our excursions into the country, Ralph and I dropped into a small roadside restaurant operated by an elderly lady. It became one of our favourite destinations. On our first visit we received a poached egg on toast, my second poached egg in England. For dessert she gave us Irish scones fresh from the oven. Now, of course, I would not rate the meal very highly except perhaps for breakfast, but for a couple of hungry cyclists, who had not had an egg for some time, it was great. On subsequent visits, we were invited into the lady's home.

Over four weeks passed before I participated in a bombing raid. In the meantime, there was not a lot for us to do. Not surprisingly, we would often hitch a ride into Nottingham or sometimes catch the bus. Nottingham was a wonderful city for service personnel; it was blessed with many lovely girls, many of whom worked in cigarette, shoe or clothing factories. While we would attend movies occasionally, our first choice was the Palais de Dance, where the dances began at seven and ended at ten, just before the buses stopped running. The dance floor was always crowded, usually with more ladies than men. Every night there would be at least one ladies' tag dance. Imagine being a young man trying to dance around the floor only to be tagged by another attractive lady. It was paradise for us except when the music stopped and it was time to make our way back to camp as best we could or stay overnight at the "Y" or a bed-and-breakfast abode. Only occasionally did I accompany a young lady to her home, because I knew if I did I would have a long walk back to my lodgings.

One of my favourite places to stay in Nottingham overnight was the Langley House, operated by Mrs. P.C. Smith. She was a good hostess, making certain we had a hearty breakfast She had two daughters, Brenda, around twelve, and a baby, both of whom I liked to see during my frequent visits as a paying guest. I was not the only airman, however, who liked staying at Langley House. There were others whom I had introduced to Mrs. Smith. Here, taken from my notes, is an account of what happened to me one night when I had come to Nottingham to attend the dance at the Palais.

Two young ladies at Langley House

*All flying was cancelled. The weather was not favourable; it would be difficult to locate enemy targets through the heavy cloud that was reported over Germany. It was not any better at Syerston and so why not spend the evening at the Palais. After getting off the bus in Nottingham, my first requirement was to find a room because I had decided to stay overnight, having received an overnight pass. Rooms were not always easy to locate and so I lost no time in heading for the Langley House. Luckily, Mrs. Smith had a vacant room. Since I might be returning late after my evening at the Palais, Mrs. Smith thoroughly briefed me as to how I could open the front door, which would likely be locked. She showed me how she had attached a string to the key, which she had hung inside the door. To get the key all I would need to do is to reach in the mail slot, find the string and pull at it.*

*In spite of the threatening weather, the Palais was full of young airmen like myself, and, as usual, many attractive girls. As always, I enjoyed dancing and talking to the girls, some of whom I had met on previous occasions. But too soon the last dance was being played and it was time to find my way to the Langley House. Because of the blackout and heavy cloud I had some difficulty locating Goldsmith Street. When I did, my next problem was to find Mrs. Smith's house. Although it was called Langley House, it looked exactly the same as its neighbours–a row of houses all joined together. My flashlight did help but not much: because of blackout regulations, except for a small hole about 1/4 inch in diameter, the lens was covered. However, I did find the mail slot and was able to pull out the key as instructed by Mrs. Smith. I opened the door and proceeded quietly up the stairs to my room so as not to awaken the other guests, using the feeble light of my flashlight to guide me. Imagine my surprise when, pointing my flashlight at my bed, I saw two persons sleeping in it. I quickly retreated. I knew immediately what had gone wrong. I was in the wrong house. Fortunately, neither of the sleepers awoke and I was able to leave the house without disturbing anyone. Next door in the mail slot I found the key I wanted and let myself in again without disturbing anyone. Not only did the houses look alike from the outside; they had, at least the part I saw, exactly the same room and stairway arrangement. I am certain the decoration was not the same; but with only the weak light of my flashlight to guide me, how was I to know? At breakfast the next morning, Mrs. Smith laughed when I told her what had happened. I don't know if she ever told her neighbours. On my next visit the key was hanging on its string. Probably so was the neighbour's.*

Although we had lost our pilot, we still wanted to fly together and tried unsuccessfully to find a pilot who would take us on. After reluctantly breaking up, it was some time before I was crewed up, leaving me with little to do in the meantime. I volunteered to fly on test flights and even managed one training flight, in which I sat in the rear turret, my only flight ever in that position. On August 3, having time on my hands, I put pen to paper to describe a typical day:

*August 3, A Typical Day.*

*Instinct it is I guess that wakens me every morning at eight. I glance at my old faithful Westclox to make certain that I am not arising too early. It is eight; I lie back feeling and appreciating the comforts of my bed as one can only do when it's time to face a new day. When I do finally climb out, it is ten after, so I dress hurriedly and pause only long enough to comb my hair and wash my hands before I stride into the mess. The breakfast is not much but it helps satisfy your appetite until lunchtime. After breakfast, if I am in the mood, I may shave. Usually I just wash up a bit and leave the shaving until noon, so if I decide to go out in the evening, I will be all set. That done, my bed made, room tidied and ship-shape, I then hop on the lady's issue bike I have been loaned, to peddle to the flights. Usually there is nothing doing there so I go to the link trainer or occasionally accompany our wireless operator on his daily inspection. Twelve o'clock brings the first half of the day to an end. I retire to the mess to read a daily paper or perhaps, if I am lucky, a letter from home. Twelve-thirty the call for lunch; everyone scrambles for the dining room. The lunch is usually good and so we leave the tables more satisfied than we did at breakfast.*

*We have until two to do as we please; we may write letters, read, or just sit and listen to the radio, as I often do. When the finger of the mess clock begins to creep to two, the crowd in the anteroom gradually thins out. I visit the flights once more. There are two compasses to be swung. We navigators, even though we now function as bomb-aimers, all go along to help and to pick up a bit of gen [information]. By four-thirty we are through. Not much use starting something else so we call it a day as far as the air force is concerned.*

*I often go out in the evenings but funds are rather low so I hang around. If I am not flying tomorrow night, I will have my fling then. This evening I will play a few games of ping-pong, or read a Toronto Star, a month old. By that time it will be about six-thirty, time for supper. After supper, I will play a few more games of ping-pong, have a sandwich at ten-thirty and then climb into my trusty bed to awaken there the next morning to a new day so much like the last one that you lose interest in time and slowly boredom sets in.*

While that may have been a typical day in August, it wasn't in September when I began flying operations with a crew, not of my choice, but of the flight commander. I had my reservations. As I said in my diary, *I don't think a lot of them [the crew] but I guess I will have to go anyway.* Actually I had no choice. It was go or be accused of "lack of moral fibre" (LMF). However, I did complete two ops (operational flights over enemy territory) with the crew without any problem. While on 61 Squadron, I flew with four other crews before I completed my tour of operations. As far as I can recall, I experienced no personality clashes.

I continued to fly as a bomb-aimer but was not particularly happy. I had joined the RCAF wanting to be a pilot. When I was turned down by the medical officer because of a vision problem, I reluctantly accepted his decision to place me in the observer category and underwent training as a gunner, a bomb-aimer and a navigator. We observers even took some training in wireless transmission. Of these three crew positions, navigator was rated the highest. Naturally I fully expected that I would serve as a navigator, with the understanding that if required in a crew I could also take on bomb-aiming responsibility. So it is not surprising that I was pleased when the flight navigation officer informed me there was a crew that needed a navigator and asked would I like to fill the vacancy. No problem! I jumped at the chance and as a consequence completed the remaining fifteen ops of my tour as navigator with a crew with which I established a very good relationship.

Looking back, I was fortunate to serve both as a bomb-aimer and a navigator. As a bomb-aimer, I had one of the best vantage points. In the turret in the nose of aircraft, I could see the 180° sector ahead of the aircraft; in the bomb bay I had the best view of what was going on below. I had to. After all, I was aiming the bombs. As a bomb-aimer I manned a two-gun turret, read maps, directed my pilot in the target area, and finally aimed and released the bombs, hopefully to strike the target.

To assist keeping on track, the navigator used Gee, a radar navigational aid. The range in which Gee could operate was limited and, hence, the navigator would depend on the bomb-aimer to provide him with pinpoints (visual land marks). When flying above cloud, astronavigation could be used or the navigator could depend on his dead reckoning, hoping that there would not be a change in the wind direction and speed he had last calculated. Astronavigation was not often used, because to ensure a reliable fix (position), the aircraft had to be flown straight and level for about six minutes. Pilots were reluctant to do this over enemy territory, as there was always the possibility of a fighter attack. Once on the final run to the target, the bomb-aimer would set the aircraft elevation on the bombsight and then direct his pilot to the target by using the words "left, steady, right," until the target was in the cross-hairs of his bombsight; at which point he would push the bomb release button saying, "bombs away!" For a few minutes the bomb-aimer's directions had priority; all other crewmembers were expected to keep their microphones off unless there was an imminent fighter attack, in which case the pilot would try to escape. If successful, he was expected to return to the target for a second run.

## CHAPTER 7

*On Operations as Bomb-Aimer*

My first op with 61 Squadron was made on August 28, 1942, to Nuremburg, Germany. This was not a successful raid. Fourteen point five percent of the aircraft, including one from our squadron, were lost and few of the bombs dropped hit the designated targets. We experienced no problems in and over the target area, but of course, like nearly all of my subsequent flights over enemy territory, we viewed other aircraft going down in flames after being caught in searchlights. We also saw explosions on the ground and large fires that had been ignited by incendiaries dropped by Bomber Command aircraft. Following this op, seven more were made in September. All of them had their hair-raising moments, as would others that I undertook before I finished my tour.

On our op to Saarbrücken following the Nuremburg flight, we were intercepted by a fighter, but either by good luck or good manoeuvring, we eluded it. Over Bremen we experienced difficulty getting out of the searchlights and as a consequence almost collided with a tethered balloon. We failed to locate the target at Wismar because of thick low cloud, so we had to return with part of our bomb load. On some flights we were airborne for long periods. For example, our Munich op took nine hours and ten minutes and our op to Danzig (now Gdansk), Poland took ten hours and fifteen minutes. Imagine what it was like to be confined in a cramped position for all that time, particularly at night. Think of the gunners and bomb-aimers like me sitting in a turret for hours with no room to stretch, with no food except perhaps a chocolate bar, with conversation over the intercom restricted, subjected to the constant noise from the engines and expected to be alert at all times. And it was cold in the rear and mid-upper turrets. And many people think flying for hours in a commercial aircraft for hours is an ordeal!

The following excerpt taken from my notes concerns our "gardening" op to Danzig. "Gardening" was the code name given to the laying of mines in harbours or enemy shipping lanes. Little opposition was usually encountered, but to drop a cylinder of high explosive on a predetermined spot called for considerable precision on the part of the aircrew.

*The Danzig Gardening Operation*

*I have always wanted to take up writing as a sort of hobby but now when I have stories to record on paper, I find I am never in the mood. However, since I am here and have a few minutes to spare, I think I should at least start to tell you about our last op, which was over Denmark and the Baltic Sea to Danzig. Let's start from the very beginning, shall we? We arose out of our cots at about two p.m. somewhat refreshed after Wednesday night's op but not as pepped-up as we should feel. Up all Wednesday night followed by six or seven hours of sleep; it should really be enough rest but it does not feel like it. Gosh, I hope we get tonight off. I don't feel so hot. Bob [our mid-upper gunner] says we're flying tonight. We may have to go on an NFT [night flying test]. Well, we are on ops all right. The skipper says we won't bother with an NFT, why I don't know. I think it is always prudent to have a test. However, he is the boss. "Hello, Redge [mid-upper gunner], are you coming over to clean your guns? You will be right over. I'll meet you there."*

*Being a bomb-aimer has its good points, but like every other position in aircrew, it has its drawbacks. Perhaps what I hate most is cleaning my two brownies [guns]. In a way it seems a waste of time. The knowledge I derive of the guns will not help me after the war; but on the other hand, if these guns did not work during a fighter attack, I might not be around to worry about my future. Now that I have run off the track of my story, I may as well tell you what a bomb-aimer does. You know of course that he aims and releases the bombs. He is also the map-reader. Anytime on an op the navigator may ask him for a pinpoint. As is usually the case, the bomb-aimer cannot help the navigator, simply because visibility is often poor, and besides, maps are decidedly difficult to read at night without a good light source.*

*It was extremely important to keep the aircraft blacked out. While the navigator did have a desk lamp, his work area was curtained off. Now you say what good is a map-reader if he is not able to assist the navigator. Well, fortunately, he does occasionally see features on the ground that he has memorized from his maps. He passes these on to the navigator, who can use them to determine if a course revision is required. When the navigator informs the pilot that they are within twenty miles of the target, the work of the bomb-aimer becomes crucial to the success of the op. He works his way down from his turret and crouches in the bomb-aimer's position over the bombsight, scanning the terrain below trying to find some feature he has memorized. When he does he directs the pilot on to the target, taking into account the defences if he is lucky enough to know where they are. When the target is in the crosshairs of the bombsight, he pushes the bomb release, taking a photograph at the same time. On their return to base the photograph will tell the tale.*

*Now, on with the story. Where was I? I was just going over to clean my guns, wasn't I? Well, let's see, I only fired a few rounds last night. I don't think I will bother cleaning them thoroughly; just shove the rod through a few times, that ought to do. Yes, they seem to be working all right. Oh, I nearly forgot the reflector sight. The guns would not be much good without it. It's OK. Have I all my tools? Yes, they are all here. Well, that's the guns–now the bomb-aimer's compartment. The bombsight seems to be in working order and the lights all work. Perhaps I ought to check the bomb panel. I'll go back and open the bomb doors. There, the warning light is on, so the electrical circuit must be all right. That finishes my inspection. I wonder how the other fellows are getting along in the back. I'd like to see a kite big enough so you could move without bending halfway over. What a life! If it isn't the main spare, it's another one. Over we go. Ah! Stan [tail gunner] hasn't started to inspect his turret. He must be helping Redge. "Hey Redge, need any help?" No answer; he is absorbed in his work. Boy, I hope he takes good care of his guns. They are the ones that count. No use me sticking around, might as well bugger off. The two of them ought to be able to clean their guns.*

*Briefing at four-thirty. Aw, we bomb-aimers are not very important anyway. I think I will have tea first. Four forty-five should be early enough. Bomb-aiming is not so bad at times. At least I would have to work a lot harder as a navigator. This tea isn't too bad. They serve pretty good meals, considering. You know, I would like to take that WAAF out sometime; she doesn't look half bad.*

*Well, that's over. Now perhaps I should hurry over to the briefing room. Goldy [our navigator] will be waiting to discuss the route with me. He may have definite landmarks for me to look out for. He is a pretty good navigator. So far we have always found the target. The briefing room doesn't seem so crowded. Can't be a very big do. Gosh, look where that string is on the wall map. I hope we have plenty of petrol. I see there are three targets. I wonder which one is ours. I'll ask Goldy.*

*We are going to Danzig. This ought to be interesting. Over Denmark, past Sweden on our port, then the target. I should be able to get pinpoints easily enough on the irregular coasts of Denmark and the Baltic Sea. I'll draw the track on my maps then examine them more thoroughly. Are there any danger areas north or south of track to look out for? No, there are none marked on the maps, so if they are up to date, we've nothing to worry about. We pass a way north of Copenhagen. I will keep that in mind in case we should find ourselves south of track. Skirting the south coast of Sweden, then another stretch of the sea, with no land near our track to the target area except, Bornholm, an island.*

*They say the target area is not heavily defended. I hope they know what they are talking about. We will have to keep away from the Danzig harbour because probably it will be protected by some strong defences. I wonder if the weather has improved since last night. Those electric storms we encountered were no fun. We are in a "col," the weatherman says. That means changeable weather and more work for the navigator to check the winds as we proceed. What's that? We may encounter electric storms over the North Sea. Why can't the weather be perfect for a change? The thought of going through huge cumulonimbus clouds, feeling the aircraft being whipped about by those strong updrafts, seeing sparks jumping from the tips of my guns, and hearing the other fellows tell us the aerials are gleaming as if they were burning is enough to make us wish we could skirt around the storm area. But enough of that. We had better listen to what the wing commander (W/Co) has to say. "You'll have a fairly easy flight," he begins. "There should not be much flak anywhere on your route and Jerry fighters will probably not bother you." I hope he knows what he is talking about. There always seems to be a lot of flak wherever we go. "You will have plenty of petrol," the W/Co says. We better have; we may need it.*

*The briefing goes on. The navigators are told what aids they can use; the pilots are given additional helpful hints, but I do not pay particular attention. I know the bomb load and the bomb stations, so there is nothing to do but study my maps a bit before briefing ends.*

*Now that briefing is over and I am on my way back to the mess, my thoughts begin to stray off track. They leave this aerodrome, the roar of engines being tested, the sound of men walking and chatting beside me and the occasional honk of some horn, to fall back to memories I had of Canada. Would I come back from this op? Was I going to complete my thirty ops without any mishap and return to Canada as I had left it? I wonder how they are getting on back home. Mother's letter should be here by now. I step in the doorway and my thoughts of home quickly give place to those of the present.*

*Flying supper is at six o'clock. That leaves me half an hour to get ready. Our meteorologist said the temperature was going to be low tonight. I'd better put on the heavy socks Bishop loaned me, and this sweater that was issued to us. It's better to be too warm than too cold. I'll wear my electric jacket, too. I hope they give us an egg for supper; I feel like one.*

*Well supper's over. It wasn't too bad although I missed the egg. They are probably saving it for breakfast. They may be able to save a few eggs that way. Who knows? I see the other fellows are on their way to the flights. Oh, hell! I forgot my locker key. Nothing for it but to walk back.*

*Boy! The flight office is certainly poorly blacked out. Our mess isn't half bad in comparison. "Hello, Redge. Hi, Goldy. Are you ready for the big do? What's the matter, Goldy? You wish you had a pack horse?" You ought to see him; his bag of navigation aids is enough in itself to carry, but he also has a parachute, a sextant and an observer compass. Why do I want to go back to navigating anyway?*

*Into the truck we climb. What a life! We're always climbing in and out of something. Come on driver, get a move on. I have to load my guns before we take off. Well, there's our kite. I hope she flies as well as she did last night. I'll crawl in first so I won't have to squeeze past anyone. Now where is the bloody light switch? Ow! That turret would have to be in the way. Over one spar, then the next, parachute first, then the maps and finally myself. What the heck am I hooked on to?*

*It's my parachute harness. It's always getting caught somewhere. It would be a hell of a note if it caught on something when I had to bail out. Now down into the bomb-aimer's compartment. Easy there, don't hit your head. Ah! We are settled in at last. It would be the last straw if the flight were scrubbed now.*

*The flight is not scrubbed. A green light is flashing at us and we are now racing down the runway. Our pilot has given the "wheels up" order and we climb, slowly circling back over the aerodrome to set course. Our wireless operator is testing the intercom, our flight engineer has been instructed by our pilot to keep an eye on the engine temperature gauges, the navigator is busy with his log, the gunners give their turrets a last check, and I prepare my maps to be ready to note any distinct landmarks that pass below us.*

*I keep my eyes on the ground, allowing my thoughts to wander a little. For all I know this may be my last flight. Will I ever see English soil again? There's Goldy asking for a pinpoint. Perhaps I can see a beacon somewhere. Ah! There's one flashing M-Mother, P-Peter. I'll look it up. It's the Farlane airfield. It's right on track. I'll let Goldy know when we pass over it.*

*Time goes quickly; it always does at the beginning of an op. The ETA [estimated time of arrival] over England's coast is almost up; I think I can see its faint outline. Is that cloud I see ahead or is it the coast? Our pilot says it's the coast, but he often mistakes a layer of stratus cloud for the coastline. Four more minutes and we should be over it. There! I see it now. It looks like we are going to cross it on track.*

*OK so far. All I have to do is keep my eyes on the sky now. The drifts Goldy obtained from the flame floats*[2] *launched by our wireless operator must have indicated to Goldy that we are on track because he has not asked our pilot to alter course. There's a light on the water ahead. It must be a flame float dropped from another one of our aircraft. I guess we are on track all right. No aircraft on the starboard side, none in front and none on the port side. I must keep my eyes moving and keep searching, especially in that dark part of the sky. If we see Jerry first we have a much better chance of eluding him. To the starboard, to the front, to the port, up, then down. I wish I had had a little more sleep last night. I don't want my eyes to get too tired. What's that below us? It's an airplane. I think it's one of our own. Yes, it is.*

[2] A flame float was a flare dropped on a body of water to enable the navigator to determine if there was change in the direction of the wind.

*On we fly. The ETA for the Danish coast has been checked and double-checked. Goldy has told me we may strike landfall north of track. I examine my maps, studying that inlet north of track, ready to recognize it if Goldy's calculations should prove correct. "Are there any defences on the section of the coast we may cross?" I ask myself as I begin to slip out of my turret. "Damn hat snap on my harness; it's always getting caught. I wish some clever person would think of a better way to get in and out of these turrets. What the heck am I caught on now? Oh, I forgot to pull out the plug of my intercom. Well, at last I am down. Now to plug in my intercom and I will be all set."*

*"Coast coming up," the skipper informs Goldy. "What, already?" I say to myself. "It can't be," but sure enough it is. I had spent a lot of time getting out of my turret. "Now, are there any distinct features on the coast? There's a large inlet to out starboard side. Let's see, it's almost like an inland lake except for one opening in the thin strip of land between it and the sea. Look below us. We are over a very irregular-shaped lake. There's no doubt about it, we are away north of track. I'll give Goldy the pinpoint." Goldy accepts the position as correct and we set course east-southeast for our next turning point. I continue to map-read, remaining in the bomb-aimer's compartment. I look for some lakes that we should pass over, but there are none to be seen. I am beginning to feel a bit worried. "I must have given Goldy a wrong position. We should have crossed those lakes long ago. Well there's one thing certain, we can't be far north or we would have passed over some water by now. We must be south. Are there any defences we are likely to fly over? No, we are OK so I won't tell our pilot what I think has happened or he will be worried. Ah! I see water ahead, a bay." Our pilot sees it and asks me to get a pinpoint. I try but I cannot find the bay on the map I am using. "Are we farther south than I think we are? Perhaps I am using the wrong map. I'll try the one that covers the area to the south." The skipper has decided we have to get a pinpoint before we go much farther. "Bomb-aimer, for heaven's sake, can't you find that bay on your map?" I reply with an ashamed, "No."*

*I hope we are not too far south; Flensburg is down there somewhere. Through the intercom our pilot is pointing out to me a long, narrow island. "Surely you can find it on your map," he remarks. It must be on this map somewhere. Love of Pete, there it is on the map as plain as day and there's the bay we just crossed farther south. "I've found it. I know where we are, pilot." He is not convinced. "Are you sure? Should that bay be north of the island?" "Yes," I answer, "it should." We're OK now. I'd better give Goldy a definite pinpoint soon or he won't believe I've found our position. I'll give him one now and another one later so he can calculate a new wind speed and direction.*

*Boy, we certainly are a way south of track. I will examine my maps again or we may run over some defended areas. There's nothing ahead except some islands. Now I see a peninsula jutting out into the sea. According to my map there is an airfield on it. I'll warn our pilot. Possibly there may be some light guns there. Ah! I was right. They have just lit up the runway. I bet they are sending up fighters to pursue us.*

*I'll keep pinpointing. It wouldn't be a joke to get off track again. Goldy is setting course for the large island some fifty miles ahead. We don't want to miss it or we will never find the harbour. Am I seeing things or is that a town lit up on our port? That must be the Swedish coast. Sure enough it is. Boy, it would be swell to return to England and find all the lights on again. But that's a futile hope; the war will never end that quickly. Those lights don't seem very far away. Perhaps, now, we are a little north of track; I'll keep a lookout on our starboard as well as straight ahead. Sure enough we are a bit north of track. We are going to pass over the northern tip of the island [Bornholm]. Goldy is setting a new course for our next landfall. If the weather holds out, this trip should be successful, providing we can outwit Jerry. I am glad we have not seen any Jerry fighters; they give me the heebie-jeebies, especially when we have a ton or two of explosives underneath us. I'll be happy when we get rid of them.*

*I'll need another map soon; I'll make sure it's handy. We should see the Polish coast in a short while. Goldy has set course for the two lakes. From there it will be up to me to pinpoint our way to the bay in which we are to lay our mines. I should not have any trouble if the cloud cover does not get any thicker. Our pilot is pointing out some lakes he sees near the coast. Yes, I believe he is right; I had not realized we were so close. Those are the lakes all right. Our pilot must agree because he has already turned to follow the coast. We are going to turn into the target area just at the root of the long peninsula. We may avoid the Jerries' defences that way. There's another inland lake ahead. I didn't think we should see another one. Let's see. Can I find it on my map? Only twenty-five miles to go. The lake is almost west of our turning point. The coast is falling away from us. The peninsula should reveal itself soon. There, I can see a dim outline of it ahead.*

*Our pilot turns on to the new course Goldy has given him when suddenly, seemingly out of nowhere, a searchlight is switched on and begins to waver up and down. "Searchlight to starboard!" is bellowed into the mikes by everyone who is in a position to see it. Our pilot kicks over the left rudder and our plane seems to contemplate for a second before it slips sideways and down. The searchlight goes out, perhaps hoping to pick us up later, but good old A for Apple soon leaves it behind.*

*We should be there soon. Only ten miles to go. I am excited. This is my responsibility. Are we too far south? I can see the harbour to the starboard and the tip of the peninsula to the port. We are to lay the mines right in the centre across the harbour entrance. "Bomb doors open," I tell our pilot. Oh! I nearly forgot. Gee! It would be terrible if I dropped them safe. "Mines fused, number one selected. Bomb gone." Goldy watches the seconds tick by on his watch. "Ready, ready, go!" I select number two and push the button. "Number two gone." In a few more seconds the third and last is gone. Our pilot jams the control forward and down we go or rather up we go. Experiencing zero or almost zero gravity, I seem to be hanging in mid-air. Holy smoke, look at that flak ship below us all lit up by the tracer she is sending at us. It is curving away to our tail. Our speed outfoxed them. We got away easily enough that time. I wonder if the defences on the peninsula will open up on us. Our pilot is not taking any chances; he is circling out of range.*

*I feel better now. Those mines ought to worry Jerry for a while. We should have an easy flight home. We have plenty of petrol, so that is one worry we will not have. After leaving the target area, I always feel sort of relieved. I guess everyone does. There is a strong temptation to relax, which is a very dangerous practice, as fighters may be waiting for us to leave the target area. However, this time there seem to be no fighters about and we continue unmolested for about an hour. The enemy on the ground often plots us for some time before he gives himself away. If his first burst of ack-ack is reasonably accurate, he usually gets in a hit, but once we know he's there, we have a reason-*

*able chance to escape. He may have been following us with radar this time because we suddenly see and feel flak bursting around us.*

*"Convoy below," someone hollers. "OK," the pilot answers as he pushes down on the control column, putting our aircraft into a steep dive. Our speed and rapid loss of altitude appears to have worked. The flak bursts are soon miles away and we are back on our original course. I have time to think now. Why did I not see that convoy before it opened up on us? I could not have been fully alert. Boy! It certainly pays to be vigilant. The engines are purring now as we pass longitude after longitude. We are getting nearer to England, but it seems we are only flying at a snail's pace; it always does on the return flight.*

*Just as I did when we crossed the Danish coast on our way to the Danzig, I gave Goldy a wrong pinpoint and, consequently, we found ourselves somewhere north of track. Exactly where I could not tell as there was a lot of cloud below us. Goldy tried to take some astro sights on Polaris, but was not successful because the air was quite bumpy. The Danish coast came into view eventually and I was able to give Goldy a pinpoint. This time it was accurate. The flight from then on was almost uneventful. I continued to provide pinpoints to Goldy until we crossed the west coast of Denmark. After that, now that we were in range of GEE, it was up to him. We were fired upon as we left the coast but the first burst of the ack-ack was some distance from us, so we had no difficulty escaping unscathed. From then on we expected our flight to be as routine as a training flight. We were tired and looking forward to feeling ground under our feet again, but that was not to be, at least not as soon as we expected. On our arrival over Syerston, because of adverse landing conditions, we were diverted to another airfield. We touched down at O545 hours, ten hours and fifteen minutes after taking off.*

There was no let-up in operational flying, but we did not let that worry us unduly. We had a job to do and we were going to do it. What choice did we have? We could refuse to fly, but that would mean we would be classified LMF (lacking in moral fibre) and demoted, shunned by all our comrades, and probably returned to Canada in disgrace. So we carried on. We sought relief by cycling in the countryside looking for interesting places to visit, dropping in on small country pubs, and occasionally even visiting Nottingham, where we might have a beer in England's oldest pub–Ye Olde Trip to Jerusalem. The Palais de Dance remained on our list as one of our favourite places. I continued to date young ladies with mixed results. Dates were nearly always made at short notice because time off depended largely on the weather. If the weather was favourable for flying, we normally had to remain close to the flight office. I did try to date a WAAF occasionally, but was rarely successful, as they were well aware of the risks we faced, so many of them did not want to become involved with a member of aircrew; better to stick with ground crew. It was unfortunate, in a way, as the WAAFs ranked high in my ratings.

Ye Olde Trip to Jerusalem

Now that I was on operations, boredom was no longer a problem. Life was anything but dull, but I still found time to write letters home almost every week and keep up correspondence with relatives and friends. In my letter home dated September 20, 1942, I refer to the Dieppe raid of August 19, which was the largest commando raid of the war, as having some benefit to the overall efforts of the Allies in spite of heavy losses in men and equipment.

*At least we know what to expect and so when another attack is made different approaches and methods will be used.*

My letters kept my parents well informed of my welfare, but I had to be careful not to say much about my activities in the air force so as not to arouse the ire of a censor. The censor I am certain would have had no problems with my comments concerning cleanliness.

*I believe that one of these days we will have to get busy. There are cobwebs in all the corners and the floor could do with a good cleaning. We have laundry hung up in two of the corners. Lately we have been doing some of our own washing.*

During one of my leaves in London, several of us were taken on a tour of the Parliament Buildings and the Daily Express building. My description of the tour taken from a letter follows:

*Our guide in the parliament buildings was a lady member of Parliament. She was quite interesting to talk to and did not appear the least bit "stuck up." It was through her that we were allowed to climb to the top of Big Ben. . . . We were shown through Westminster Hall, where the present king and queen were crowned. She showed us the cupboard where Guy Fox was found hiding. We viewed the Thames River from the balcony to which, years ago, prisoners were taken from a boat to be tried before the King's Bench. Our next stop was the House of Commons, where we saw the throne, or at least what I always imagined to be the throne, and we were shown the speakers' platform. Before we left, the lady MP gave us her views on current developments that were of interest to us and she invited us to come back sometime when Parliament was in session. . . . The tour of the Daily Express building was almost as interesting. We were shown every part of the building and how each machine was operated. We learned that Mrs. Roosevelt was in England an hour before notice of her arrival was broadcast. I swiped a newspaper so I could read tomorrow's news today.*

That I was changing my view of English girls is illustrated by this excerpt taken from another letter written home after I had returned to Syerston from London.

*Last evening as I was standing beside the road waiting for a lift, a girl whom I had met some weeks previously with an airman friend stopped to talk with me. She was cycling home after working in her father's sugar beet fields all day. You should have seen her. She was mud from head to foot. She had on rubber boots many sizes too large yet she did not seem embarrassed in the least. I never pictured an English girl working on a farm. I did not think they had what it takes, but now I am forced to change my opinion. Imagine cutting off beet tops in the mud up to your ankles in a slow, steady drizzle. Girls who do this work without complaining certainly have my respect.*

To boast our morale while we were on operations and to help us to return to the real world, we were given generous leave benefits. I often used my leave to visit relatives on my mother's side. I always received a wonderful welcome and they tried their best to entertain me. I struck up a warm friendship with a cousin, which I maintained until she passed away a few years ago.

However, as already noted, I did sometimes spend leave with airmen friends. It was always my intention to behave in a manner that, if it did not enhance the image of Canadians in Britain, it at least did not degrade that image. However, on the night of September 16, 1942, I fell off my perch. I was in Manchester with Allen, a navigator with whom I had flown several ops as a bomb-aimer. Two days later I wrote an account of that night:

*The king's uniform has changed me–whether for the better or worse it is not for me to judge. You, who knew me before the war, can answer that. I cannot let the night of the 16th/17th go by without leaving an account so you can guess how far I have wandered off the beaten paths of those of you who possess high moral standards. Before I begin, let me say I never intend to allow this to happen again, but who knows, this despicable behaviour may have a stronger hold on me than I realize.*

*This story begins early Wednesday evening when Allen met me in front of the YMCA in Manchester. This was our last night out before our leave ended, so you can easily guess what we had in mind: A night of drinking, to drink until we felt good and had put aside our thoughts of war. (Before I continue, may I say that had I been alone, I would probably never have participated in such disreputable behaviour. I am not blaming my companion; I should not drink with him.) As the evening rolled by we drank glass after glass of beer. The time came when I thought we should attend a dance. I was satisfied and felt in the mood for good music and a lovely dancing partner. Allen found nothing to his taste so I, always being an obliging sort of fellow, left with him. We visited a pub and there from a young man we learned of the rough areas of the city. We were on our way when we ran into two girls. To our stuporous minds, they looked interesting, and after receiving their consent escorted them home. We soon found there would be no joy, so quickly left.*

*Now our main goal was to find a place to continue our drinking orgy. All the pubs were closed but we still had the rough section of Manchester to visit. We saw a light shining from a doorway and heard music. It was only a baker's shop. We tried our hands at making doughnuts but were not very successful. Our interest soon wore off and we left the shop carrying two of the most delicious doughnuts I had ever eaten. However, that did not help us forget the object of our hunt. Now our interest thoroughly aroused, we explored every doorway that gave some indication that it was not just the doorway to an ordinary home. At one door that was opened to our knock, Allen had no choice but to ask the way to some street he remembered having seen, because the man who opened the door did not in any way look like someone who would be providing beer after the pubs had closed.*

*By now you are saying that we must have been well and truly intoxicated, but I seem to have remembered everything that we did. That should show that some of our senses were with us at any rate. No luck at the first fish and chip shop, but at the second, after making inquiries, a quiet, rather dull-looking man dressed in civvies said he would lead us to a place where we could drink as long as we liked. I had never been to one of these places so I thought the experience would do me no harm and anyway I could not let Allen down. A long walk it was before our new-found friend gently knocked on a door of what seemed like an ordinary home. The door opened slowly and we heard a woman in what was almost a whisper say, "Who's there?" "It's me Jock," was the reply. "Who's that with you?" "There's only two soldiers." (Apparently Jock could not tell an airman from a soldier.)*

*And so we entered a dive, a place you read about but never visit. Except for the empty beer bottles, the place seemed normal. We sat down in chairs beside the fireplace and began to drink for what I thought was a short time but we drank on and on, bottle after bottle. It was five before we decided to leave. But we were not the only drinkers. There were two girls, one accompanied by her mother and the other presumably was a friend. The lady who opened the door for us, and who I assume owned the house, also drank with us. The two girls seemed to be respectable but the mother I imagine had had* her *day, although at first glance she looked somewhat decent. After all the beer we had consumed, the fact that we managed to stand upright and were able to walk was a miracle. Next morning we had severe headaches and did not fully recover until the following day. I think the beer we drank was bad. I never thought that I would ever consume so much beer. I hope the experience will have taught me a lesson.*

Letters from home continued to arrive every week or two. If not a letter from Mother, there would be one from my father or brother, or occasionally from an aunt or my grandparents. Letters did a lot to boost our morale, but probably it was the parcels that we enjoyed most. By September 30, 1942, I had received twenty-three parcels and forty letters from my parents. Here are some excerpts taken from my letters home that will give you some idea of the role the parcels played in my life.

*March 18, 1942*

*I hate to bother you again but I need some underwear shorts and a pair of black leather gloves. If you have already sent me the shorts, don't bother about the gloves because my present pair will last until summer.*

*April 9, 1942*

*I don't need canned foods as much as I do underwear shorts and a shirt. I could use a tie also.*

*April 23, 1942*

*Number 8 parcel reached me last Saturday. The Easter egg was very good; the shorts fit well and so does the shirt.*

*June 10, l942*

*I think that all the letters and parcels you have sent me have arrived. I have your letter of May 8 in front of me. Thanks for the shorts. I have four pair now, which should be enough. The socks are appreciated.*

(You would think the underwear problem was solved, but it wasn't.)

*August 20, 1942*

*The shorts you sent me have shrunk a bit so are rather tight. I could do with a few more pairs but larger this time, size 38.*

(In actual fact, I had not realized it at the time, but the reason the shorts were tight was because I had put on weight.)

*January 14, 1943*

*Your letter number sixty-three written on December 17 arrived here yesterday. I am glad the shoes have been sent as I had to send mine in for repair a few days ago. They are about all in. I will not have to worry so much about shoes now because I have just been promoted to warrant officer, which means I should be issued with a pair.*

*May 19, 1943*

*The shirt and shorts you are sending will be appreciated but now that I have clothing coupons, it is not necessary for you to send me any more clothes.*

As a non-commissioned officer, I was provided with a uniform and other clothing. I don't recall why I felt it necessary to bother my parents for boxer shorts nor are there any clues in my diary as to why I could not have drawn them from stores. Shoes of course were a special category. We were issued heavy boots, which were a bit unwieldy on the dance floor. Accordingly, whenever we left camp, we would wear shoes, if we had any.

During October 1942 we flew almost every day, either on an op, undergoing special flying training, or doing NFTs (night flying tests). It was during this period that I was asked if I would like to transfer back to navigation. As already noted above, I was pleased, because since graduating as an observer I had always thought of myself as a navigator. But it would be some time before I would actually sit in the navigator's position, keeping the pilot on track.

Low-formation flying took a lot of our time. We obviously were being prepared for a special op that would take place in daylight. One day over ninety Lancasters were involved in low-flying exercises. Imagine flying on a daylight raid in formation, as was the practice of American bombers, but without a fighter aircraft escort. Understandably, we were apprehensive.

On October 16, we participated in a raid on Cologne, in the Ruhr Valley, which, from my vantage point in the front turret, was a failure. It turned out I was right. Some time later, we learned that many of our bombs had been dropped on a large decoy fire ignited by the enemy. Anyway, the next day our daylight target was a large

En route to Le Creusot

factory and a power station in Le Creusot, about halfway between Lyon and Dijon. The factory was a large producer of heavy guns, railway engines and it was thought possibly also of tanks and amoured cars.

By 1200 hours we were airborne and within a short time were part of a force of ninety-four Lancasters flying around the Brittany peninsula, to cross the French coast between St. Nazaire and La Rochelle. Flying most of the 300 miles at treetop level was exciting. From my perch in the front turret I had an all-encompassing view of the passing countryside. Never did I think that many years later in my retirement I would participate in a cycling tour in the same area over which we were flying. I could see many of the aircraft that were flying in loose formation with us. Other than completing an op in daylight and at low level with ninety-four other Lancasters, the flight was uneventful. According to my diary:

*We bombed our target [the transformer-power station] successfully and shot it up on the way back. Only one kite [aircraft] was lost. There were no Jerry fighters or ack-ack on the way in. On the whole the flight was well planned by Bomber Command.*

The following day we learned that the lost aircraft was from our squadron. It was reported that the crew had bombed the transformer station at such a low level that their aircraft had crashed into the station. While we had thought that this had been a successful attack, the photographs later proved that much of the bombing had fallen short of the targeted plants.

Surprisingly, as least to us as a crew, we were informed the day after our return from Le Creusot that we had six days' leave. Presumably this was because our pilot had completed his tour of operations and our flight commander would need time to find other crews for us. So with no time to prepare for a break, I chose London as my destination. I was not disappointed, as the following account written on October 25 indicates I enjoyed my visit:

*No Canadian, after visiting London, can say that the Brits do not appreciate Canadians who have volunteered to serve in the armed forces. Too many Canadians seem to feel they are regarded as tools of the Empire by the Brits. Visit London. There, you will receive hospitality at its best. Clubs that offer accommodation to Canadian forces often equal to that provided by the best hotels are situated all over greater London. Not only do they offer accommodation, but also excellent meals; and, above all, entertainment for any disposition. Tours are arranged in interesting and celebrated parts of London. It is a fact that Canadian visitors often are able to visit places that that the average Londoner has never seen. To a Canadian, London is a city of opportunities. You see as many places in a week as it would take months to cover in peacetime.*

# CHAPTER 8

*Promoted to Navigator*

On my return, I was told definitely that I was now classed as a navigator and would have an American–Terry Goodwin–as my pilot. Terry, who had joined the RCAF in February 1941, not long after I had joined, had not yet had any Lancaster flying experience. Consequently, on November 4, 1942, we were posted to a conversion flight at Swinderby, an airfield within cycling distance of Syerston so that Terry could get the necessary qualifications. On one occasion, we participated in a mock air battle with some Beau fighter aircraft. Terry, based on my experiences with other pilots, impressed me. I was beginning to feel good that fate had put us together. He was well liked by other airmen and the other members of our crew. Besides flying with Terry, I attended a number of lectures on various subjects to do with flying, such as astronavigation and bombing techniques. In addition we were instructed on how we should handle ourselves if ever we were taken prisoner of war, on the role of the RAF, and on military action being undertaken in other theatres of war.

A day before our crew would rejoin 61 Squadron, which was good news as far as we were concerned, the wing commander confirmed that Terry and I had been recommended for commissions. While we welcomed the news, it would be some time before we would don the uniform of a pilot officer.

Since we had left Syerston, many new crews had joined 61 Squadron and its sister squadron, 106. Hence, accommodation was limited with the consequence that we had difficulty in finding a bunk. Ralph, my former roommate, now had a new roommate and so I could no longer share a room with him. It was several weeks before Terry and I were settled in a room of our own.

Although I was pleased with my new role, I was apprehensive about my navigation skills. It had been six months since I had last sat in the navigator's position. Finally, a few days before my first op with my new crew, we were sent on two cross-country exercises. While they did assist me to regain my confidence, on both occasions we were recalled to base before completion of the exercises. Nonetheless, I was now prepared to take on my responsibilities as navigator and was reasonably confident that I would be able to carry out my task in my curtained-off compartment directly behind Terry and our flight engineer, Sergeant Lewis.

Our first op, which took place on December 9, was to Turin (Torino) in northern Italy. While it would involve over seven hours of flying, crews for the most part were not overly concerned. Turin was not a heavily defended target like those along the Ruhr River, which some of us called Happy Valley, but not because there was any happiness involved–just the opposite.

At about 1700 hours, our crew climbed into a truck to take us to our aircraft. Like all the other navigators, I was loaded down with gear including a Dalton Computer, one of the navigator's most important aids. While this hand-held instrument did assist the navigator to calculate wind speed and direction, under present-day terminology it would never have been called a computer.

As already noted, by far the most important aid to navigation was GEE, a cathode-ray receiver, which sat on one side of the navigator's worktable. Through use of GEE, the navigator could quickly and accurately determine his aircraft's position. Unfortunately, its range was limited to 400 miles under ideal conditions, which rarely happened. The enemy, through studying the GEE equipment in downed aircraft, soon found a way to jam the transmitted electronic pulses, reducing its range drastically.

Our crew took off sometime after all the other aircraft had become airborne. Our plane had not been fully serviced by the time we arrived at the dispersal site. Finally, after waiting around for about forty minutes, we climbed on board. Terry and Lewis checked their instrument panels and revved up the engines, and we slowly moved to the takeoff position. A few of our support personnel stood at the edge of the runway ready to wave us off. Sitting at my worktable, I experienced a few seconds of concern. After all, this was going to be my first op as a navigator. Would I be able to get us to the target and back? It was going to be a long flight and I could experience some difficulty in keeping on track.

The pinpoint given to me by our bomb-aimer as we passed over the French coast confirmed my skills; at least so far we were on track. However, he could not get a pinpoint over central France, so I decided to use the sextant. It was not an easy instrument to use. I had to find my way back to the astrodome and at the same time ensure I remained in contact with Terry. It was most important that the aircraft fly straight and level for about six minutes while I was shooting the stars. Over enemy territory, pilots felt vulnerable. They wanted to be ready to take evasive action at all times, because fighters could appear out of nowhere and ack-ack bursts and searchlights could suddenly light up the sky.

Having taken the shots I needed, it took me another six minutes or so get back to my table and plot the fix, referring to astro-tables. I was then able to confirm that the wind I was using was keeping us on track. Fortunately, there were no significant wind changes for the remainder of the flight to Turin, so my dead reckoning brought us right into the target area. Due to our late departure from Syerston, we were concerned that we would arrive late over the target area, alone, and hence vulnerable to ack-ack fire.

Fortunately, there were still other aircraft over the target area and the defences of Turin were not nearly as heavily concentrated as those at German target areas. So we had little difficulty aiming our bombs at our designated target. According to information gathered after the op, this was a successful raid. Of the 133 aircraft that took part, only one was lost.

We had bombed the target. Now with a bit of luck and accurate navigation on my part we would be back in our beds in a few hours. But that was not to be. As we crossed the French coast, suddenly, without warning, coastal ack-ack tracers started to stream in our direction. We were hit. Our port outer engine sputtered and ceased to provide power. However, having one engine down was not the end of the world. Without a bomb load, the Lanc could maintain altitude with little difficulty. Unluckily in our case, Terry and our engineer could not get the propeller to stop turning. In pilot's terms they could not feather the propeller, causing the aircraft to yaw and creating extra drag. Still we were not overly worried. If the other three engines continued to provide full power we could return to base. But our troubles were not over yet. When we arrived over

Syerston, we found we could not make voice contact; our radio/transmitter was dead. So there was nothing we could do but circle the airfield for thirty-five minutes until our control tower made wireless contact with us authorizing us to land–but at Swinderby, because of landing problems at our own field.

As we completed our approach to the runway at Swinderby, a red light flashed indicating we had to abort the landing. There apparently was an obstruction on the runway; perhaps another crew were having trouble moving their aircraft out of the way. As Terry tried to regain height in order to circle the field and wait for a second opportunity to try an approach, I noticed that our airspeed was dropping fast and the aircraft was not climbing. I knew then we were in real trouble. I seem to remember feeling the aircraft shudder a bit. It probably was the tops of trees we hit as we came closer to the ground. The aircraft eventually came to a shuttering stop accompanied by crashing sounds. We were on the ground. Knowing that the aircraft might catch on fire, we scrambled like rats out of a flooded hole. Tom, our tail-gunner, was the last and we had to pry him out of his turret, which had been torn from the fuselage. Fortunately, there were no serious injuries, although both Terry and Tom had sustained cuts to their foreheads. We had landed on the edge of a village three miles from the airfield.

Three of us left to try to get help while the rest of the crew stayed with the aircraft. I knocked on the door of the first house we came to. It was answered by a man in his nightgown. When we told him there was a Lancaster a short distance away, he seemed to have trouble believing us. I asked him to let me use his phone. He said he did not have one and directed us to the pub. So we had to wake up the proprietor. He was most concerned that we were all OK, and offered to phone the base while I brought the remainder of the crew to the pub. On our return we were given drinks and made comfortable until a truck arrived. While I don't remember much of the interrogation by the intelligence officer I do remember him criticizing us for not having one of our crew stay on guard at the aircraft. After all we had gone through, I thought he was being a bit presumptuous. There were other personnel that could well have assumed that responsibility.

Following our return to Syerston, all of us were asked to report to the MO (medical officer). As a consequence everyone, except me, was given a forty-eight hour leave. Presumably I did not reveal any need to have a break after our crash. During the next three days, I swung a compass, did other miscellaneous chores for the squadron navigation officer, and spent some time in the intelligence office.

On December 14, we flew an NFT with Terry for the first time since the crash. I was a bit concerned but soon realized that the crash had not affected Terry's flying skills. The following day we took off on a mine-laying op from which we were recalled because of adverse weather. On our return we were criticized. Although we had released our mines *safe* so they would not explode on impact, we had dropped them close to allied shipping lanes off England's coast.

All members of the crew, except me, had been promised leave. They made an appointment with the squadron commanding officer to request that the promise be kept. They were successful and since I could not fly without a crew, I also was given leave. To have leave at Christmas time meant a lot to the English members of the crew. Now, where was I going to spend Christmas? At my Great Aunt Bessy's, why not?

On December 20, I left Nottingham by train hoping to arrive at my Aunt Bessy's home near Cheltenham at a reasonable hour, but it seemed everyone was trying to get home for Christmas. As the crow flies it was not a long journey, but the trains took a much less direct route, and there was a delay of two hours between trains in Derby. Standing in the corridor most of the time made the journey feel longer than it actually was. Rather than arriving late at my aunt's home, I rented a hotel room in Cheltenham.

I will never forget this Christmas. It was so quiet. There were few signs anywhere that Christmas Eve was but a few days away. There were no decorations in Aunt Bessy's home, no presents waiting to be opened, and no indication of special preparations for Christmas dinner. Fortunately there was John, Aunt Bessy's grandson, and his parents to make my visit more enjoyable. I also was able to visit another relative and his family who lived nearby on a farm. As indicated in my letter home of December 24, I particularly enjoyed John's company. About twelve years old, he seemed to enjoy going for walks with me and attending movies, which was about all there was for us to do:

*I suppose you will be glad to know I am spending Christmas at Aunt Bessy's. It is very quiet here. I do miss my mates. I have often wondered if I could spend a few days quietly as I used to on our farm without feeling out of sorts. I admit time has gone slowly at certain times, but John, Aunt Bessy's grandson, has gone for walks with me and to a couple of movies. Tuesday morning he took me for a walk across some fields, through woods and finally up some hills. The grass was wet and there was a lot of mud but I didn't mind; it was good to be out in the open with no worries, to slip and skid in the mud and to swear silently to myself. I tried to show John how I could catwalk on a fence railing. I slipped and fell in the mud. John had a good laugh; I joined in as soon as I regained my composure.*

*You may wonder what the Wilcoxes are doing tonight. They are spending the evening as they usually do, sitting around the fireplace, the only source of heat in their home. Aunt Bessy is knitting. Her daughter and Sam, her daughter's husband, and John are listening to a "March of Time" radio program. John is not at all excited about Christmas. He has nothing to be excited about. The English people do not know how to celebrate Christmas. No one has wished me a Merry Christmas. When I wished people I met a Merry Christmas, they looked surprised.*

I should mention that one of the reasons there were so few signs of Christmas was the need to exchange ration coupons for gifts and ornaments. In another letter I stated that:

*Shops over here are not well stocked but much better than you would expect in a country at war. Toys are hard to get and those that are for sale are very expensive. Christmas shoppers have a difficult job on their hands as they must give up coupons for so many of the things they would like to buy.*

I departed my aunt's home in the early afternoon of Boxing Day and arrived back at the sergeants' mess just in time to enjoy the tail end of a party that may well have been going on and off for two days. No operational flights took off from Syerston during Christmas.

Life went on. Bob Bird, a member of my original crew, informed me that he had a problem, unfortunately not a rare one in the RAF.

He had been visiting a young lady in Newark for some time and now she was pregnant. He was concerned as to what he should do. Unfortunately, I was not able to give him much help. Anyway, his problem, as far as he was concerned, was solved, albeit not the way he would have liked. On January 17, 1943, Bob's crew was reported missing. He had been shot down over Dorberitiz, a suburb of Berlin, the only aircraft lost out of the 201 that had taken part in the Berlin raid. All members of the crew were killed. We had been on this op to Berlin also and returned safely encountering very little flak and seeing only one enemy fighter. We eventually learned that half of the flak units were outside of Berlin taking part in a course.

The following article on this raid was taken from a Toronto paper.

> ***London, Jan. 17 (CP)***[3]
>
> Many Canadians attached to Lancaster bomber squadrons were with the attacking force that swarmed over Berlin Saturday night to send block-busting high explosives and thousands of incendiary bombs crashing into the German capital. No RCAF aircraft took part in the raid, however.
>
> Like the returning British airmen, the Canadians expressed surprise at the lightness of the resistance offered by the Nazis during the long trip from Britain. Keil and Cologne were a lot worse said W/O John Patterson of Bobcaygeon, Ontario, a 21-year old navigator. "We have never taken so long over our bombing run as we did last night. The flak wasn't bad and we saw only one searchlight."
>
> Patterson, a schoolteacher in peacetime, was praised highly by his skipper, an English sergeant, for the manner in which he found the target in spite of heavy clouds. "He took us straight over the target without getting a pinpoint on route and we arrived dead on," the sergeant said. "It was so thick along the way that you could not see a thing to pinpoint on. It was super navigation."

At about this time I wrote the following article.

> **They Bombed the Target**
>
> The book I was reading ceased to interest me. I heard the dull throb of many engines overhead. I had heard the same sound

[3] Note: There are two errors in this newspaper report. I was not a schoolteacher nor was Terry Goodwin, our pilot, an English sergeant. He was an American.

many times and it always attracted my attention. Perhaps because it was so easy, from my bed, to picture myself navigating in one of those planes.

I did not realize it then but Sam and his crew were in one of those aircraft on their way to bomb an Italian port. I knew all his crew but only Jim, the bomb-aimer, and Don, the navigator, intimately. I met Jim for the first time at the advanced training unit where, he, Don and I trained. For the next six months, we remained together most of the time. They were like everyone else; they had their faults. Jim liked his beer and Don liked his girls. Sam did not come into the picture until the three of us graduated to an operational training unit. Joe chose him as his pilot–the reason? Well, in Sam's opinion, beer was the essence of life. They chose Don to be their navigator, perhaps because he too, when there were no attractive girls about, did not object to the odd "noggin." As a team, they were tops. On their squadron, as a crew, they ranked with the best. On the ground they respected no one any more than they had to, but in the air their discipline was perfect.

It must have been or they would never have returned from Italy that night. Jim told me later that the flight over France to the target was no different from any of the others they had completed. They saw the usual beacons flashing near their parent aerodromes and the mysterious twinkling lights that we occasionally see over French territory. They may have been lights cast upward by lanterns carried by farmers tending their stock. We liked to think of them as patriots beckoning to us, wishing us well. The lights of Geneva shone beside Lake Geneva as quiet and serene as ever. The towering peaks of the Alps reflected the cold light of the moon.

The Alps had just been crossed when Jim told me one of the engines had "packed up." The gremlins had been working on the magneto. The target was not heavily defended; only a bit of light flak was coming up but this must have been one of Sam's unlucky nights. One of the remaining three engines was "knocked out." Sam could have jettisoned his bombs and turned for home but he was not going to waste them. He pressed on. They were scared, Jim said. He could feel the tension. What if another engine "packed up"? Neither of the remaining engines did. Jim dropped his bombs on the target. Their troubles were not over. The aircraft had to be nursed home and there was not enough power to climb over the Alps. There was only one alternative: to take the longer route over southern France along the Spanish border.

All the way home they were an inviting target, almost a sitting one for fighter aircraft. They were like shipwrecked sailors in a dinghy with a hole in it, praying that it will stay afloat long enough to carry them to a distant island. The whole crew knew that only with God's help, would they get back. They all shouted for joy when they saw a fighter escort in the dim light of early morning coming to guard them on the last leg of that long flight home. They had done the impossible. The air officer commanding showed his appreciation of the achievement by writing his opinion of each member of the crew in their log books.

When this war is over some mothers will be very proud of those log books because they may be the only record they will have of their sons' exploits. You see following their next op, there was only one more entry after that of the air officer commanding: "Missing in Action."

Mother in one of her letters asked for information on tiny mysterious men that had been reported accompanying us on our flights–gremlins. I had this to say:

*Those little men you speak of are called gremlins. I am of the opinion that there are both Allied and enemy gremlins. Different crews have reported gremlins in their engines that caused them to stutter and backfire until they finally stopped. One crew had two engines fail by enemy gremlins but our Allied gremlins put up a grim fight and were able to keep the two other engines going. As the aircraft neared the coast, more Allied gremlins climbed on board, and so the aircraft was soon out of harm's way and reached base safely.*

In letters home on March 4 and 10, 1943, I again referred to gremlins:

*The gremlins have been working lately. An aircraft detailed to bomb a German city turned around in circles and no one yet seems to know the reason. They are blaming the magnetic gremlins who seem to take great enjoyment in playing with aircraft compasses. . . . Last week I told you about the magnetic gremlin. We have had trouble with a new type of gremlin lately, the weather gremlin. They surprise us sometimes by turning the wind right around to the opposite direction we expected it to come from. They play queer tricks on aircrews taking them over areas they had not wanted to cross.*

Sick again. This time with little warning. On January 18, I was lying in a hospital bed minus my appendix and sharing a large ward with fourteen other airmen in the armed force's hospital about twenty miles from Syerston. My stay in the hospital, which stretched to February 2, as you can visualize was not particularly pleasant. I was not at all happy having to stay in the hospital, as I wanted to get back with my crew. I did have visitors occasionally, including two padres and an elderly lady who brought me chocolates and magazines. Eventually, when I had recovered sufficiently to be discharged there was some difference of opinion among the medical staff as to whether I should be sent to a convalescent home or given leave to recuperate. I wanted leave. The nursing sisters were on my side and I was soon wondering where I would spend my two weeks' leave. One of the medical officers suggested Edinburgh and/or Glasgow.

So, 1420 hours, February 5, found me on the Edinburgh station platform exhausted after a very tiresome journey. What a way to start convalescence. To add to my discomfort, I had difficulty finding a place to call home for the next few days. Fortunately, the Victoria League Club was able to find a bed for me in its annex and I settled down to enjoy a wonderful time both in Edinburgh and Glasgow. Compared to the cities I had already visited on previous leaves–Liverpool, Birmingham and London–Edinburgh was a jewel. Glasgow's friendliness, on the other hand, more than made up for its dowdy appearance. Princess Street, Edinburgh's main thoroughfare, is one of the world's most beautiful streets. Across the ravine is the historic Royal Mile, which leads from Edinburgh Castle on Castle Rock to Holyrood Castle. Along with a guide and several other airmen, I walked the Mile, touring both of the castles on our way, before ending up at the Wishing Well. The following day we toured St. Giles Cathedral and visited the home of John Knox, who led the Protestant Reformation in Scotland in the sixteenth century. Not all my time was spend on tours, however. I enjoyed Scottish dancing on two occasions, one of which was at a party especially arranged for nineteen of us Canadians.

The following quote from a letter written home on February 15 confirms that I also had a good time in Glasgow:

*I am having a wonderful time in Glasgow going to a party every night. It is the first time I have ever been to so many parties. They were all enjoyable with plenty to eat. Last night we had a party here at the club attended by girls who work in different overseas clubs throughout the city. It was well planned; everyone enjoyed themselves. We danced Scottish old-time dances, which I enjoy more than modern dancing. We also played games, which brought smiles to everyone's faces.*

While in Glasgow, I was so busy having a good time that I only managed to take part in two tours–one to biscuit plant and the other to see the ruins of Bothwell Castle, which was built by the Earl of Bothwell (James Hepburn), the third husband of Mary, Queen of Scots. Of the two, it is not surprising that I enjoyed the biscuit plant tour more, possibly because I was able to sample all the cookies as they were removed from the ovens and to enjoy a short concert arranged specially for us by some of the young female employees.

Upon returning to Syerston, I was happy to learn that my crew had not gone missing, as I had heard on my way through Nottingham. I was reinstated as their navigator and was glad to be back sharing a room with Terry. But I still had five days' leave remaining. I had had enough of parties and riding in slow-moving trains; besides I was running short of money. So I requested permission from the squadron engineer to work with the maintenance crews. I enjoyed climbing around the engines and working with the crews; under close supervision, of course, as I knew little about aircraft engines.

After completing my convalescent leave and passing a medical exam, I was reinstated with my crew. On our first flight together, which was from an airfield where we had been sent to pick up an aircraft, we experienced a hair-raising experience. We encountered RAF fighters who indicated by their maneuvers they would like to show us how they would attack an aircraft like ours. Terry did not discourage them. Soon he was doing everything he could to get out of their line of sight. The fun continued until we heard a sharp crack. The rudder bar had broken, presumably from the pressure Terry put on it while he was twisting and turning the aircraft. It should never have broken; it must have been defective. In any case without full rudder control, landing safely would be difficult. Fortunately, our ingenious flight engineer found some wire that he used to make a temporary repair.

Over the next eleven days, we took part in seven operations. Losses varied from 1.1% over St. Nazaire on the French coast to 5.3% over Berlin. Normally the losses were around 2.4%, which seems small, but soon adds up. An idea of the number of airmen reported missing from a single raid can be deduced from the Cologne raid of February 26, 1943. Of the 2,843 airmen participating, sixty-five did not return. If the remaining airmen continued to participate in similar raids until they completed their tour of thirty ops or were reported missing, there would only have been 893 left on the squadrons. Or stated in percentage terms, over 68% would have been reported missing or killed in action.

Our ground crew, 61 Squadron

As stated in my diary:

*The bombing of Cologne apparently was successful. There were huge fires burning when we released our bombs. The defences seem to have been outfoxed and were using their searchlights haphazardly. We encountered no fighters. Our squadron has done well this week, sending over twenty eight-aircraft with no boomerangs [uncompleted missions] and no losses.*

In spite of our high losses over Berlin, the op was considered a partial success. According to subsequent reports, although many bombs missed their target, there was extensive damage to railway shops and factories. In my diary I considered the op a success:

*We could see fires burning over 150 miles away on our homeward flight. Our route took us directly back to base over the heart of Germany. Passed through a number of searchlight and fighter belts to reach the Dutch coast thirty miles south of track. We brought back a good photograph [taken on our bombing run].*

Our op to Essen on March 5 was not completed. We returned to base because one of our engines cut out due to a faulty magneto. You would have thought we might have criticized our ground crew on our return. On the contrary, we appreciated of the effort the crew made to ensure that our aircraft, "M for Mother," was kept in top condition. There had not been any indication of a magneto problem during the night flying test we made prior to the op takeoff.

The last op made prior to our crew going on leave was to Nuremburg. Owing in part to poor visibility, many bombs missed their target. Nonetheless, several factories and railway installations were hit. The following account of an airman's horrendous experience as a consequence of this raid is taken from *The Bomber Command War Diaries*, by Martin Middlebrook and Chris Everitt:

> Sergeant D.R. Spanton, a mid-upper gunner of a 7 Squadron Stirling, had a fortunate escape on this night. After his aircraft crossed the English coast on the return flight, Spandon realized that he was the only man still in the plane. The remainder of the crew, a new crew in this Pathfinder Squadron, had bailed out earlier, possibly because of a suspected fuel shortage, and the pilot left the plane flying on automatic pilot. Spanton had not heard the order [to bail out]. He parachuted

safely over Kent and the empty Stirling crashed into the Thames estuary. The remainder of the crew, presumably thinking they were parachuting over France, had actually come down in the sea and were all drowned. Sergeant Spanton went on to fly a further 12 operations but his plane was lost on the night of 24/25 June 1943 in a raid on Wuppertal and the presence of his name on the Runnymede Memorial probably indicates that he died in the sea on that occasion.

It was about this time that our favourite dog was taken from us. He was named "Wimpey" after the Wellington two-engine bomber, by the crews who flew in it. Here is the story I wrote about Wimpey.

**Wimpey**

It was late. As I was taking some water from the boiler room, I heard a scratching in the adjoining room. A sorrowful-looking mutt looked intently up at my face. He wagged his short stubby tail and, coming closer, he sniffed my trousers. Then he seemed to lose interest. He turned away and walked slowly to the door, turning every few steps to look beseechingly up at me. I had not intended to let him out, but somehow he sneaked past me. I saw him disappear around the corner of his master's barrack block.

For the last week Wimpey had been puzzled. He could not understand where his master had gone. Whenever I whistled to him, he would bound towards me, then stop short, his face betraying his bewilderment: "That's not my master's whistle–or is it?" He would sniff my trousers and then turn away to continue the search for his master.

Wimpey is meant, I believe, to be a Scotty, but he looks like a mutt. He is not handsome. That is probably why I did not notice him any more than I did the other dogs that hung around 5 Site. Not until I knew his master did I learn to like Wimpey. In his master's company he would not even look at me, but when his master was away, I gradually was able to make friends with him. Wimpey loved to play with the medicine ball in the crew room. To him the ball was a living thing. He would touch it; then when it moved, he would jump back barking–I should say more like whimpering. He would become so excited that he would forget how to bark and would only yelp, seemingly in terror. He would play with the ball until

> his legs would not support him, or until we became fed up with his barking and yelping.
>
> He has not been in the crew room for a long time now. There is no one to take him there. He will soon be given an honourable discharge; in a few days he will be on his way to his master's home where he has a new job waiting for him. His mistress will be glad to have him as playmate for the new member of the now fatherless family.

With another leave of seven days ahead of me, I was at loss as to where I would spend it. Having returned from convalescent leave a few weeks before, I was not prepared for more time off. Besides, I was short of funds, particularly since I had arranged for a significant part of my salary to be deposited in my Toronto bank account. I decided to visit Major Reg Lecoustre and his wife Popeye. While I was on leave in the Lake District, they had given me an open invitation to visit them at their home near Preston, in Lancashire. So with almost no notice, I informed them I was coming to see them. Had I known that they were living in a one-bedroom apartment of a farm home they shared with the owner, I don't suppose I would have decided to spend part of my leave with them. I could have visited my aunt and uncle in Liverpool. In any event although I shared the bedroom with Reg and Popeye had to sleep on the sofa in the living room, I had a very enjoyable holiday. I never did determine why Reg called his wife Popeye; perhaps it was because she had lovely, slightly protruding eyes.

I was able to sleep in every morning, and to wake up to a sumptuous breakfast. Reg would have long since left for work, so I spent most of my time in the company of Popeye discussing farming in Canada. As a land army volunteer, Popeye did everything from driving a tractor, to forking manure and milking cows. We would have long conversations about the different farming methods practiced by our two countries. Occasionally, I would go on a long walk, enjoying the sunny, warm weather. One of the Lecoustres' favourite haunts was the Half-Way House, a pub in Preston where, not surprisingly, we spent a couple of evenings. I liked meeting the local people.

Many of the Preston area farmers were heavily involved in the dairy industry. As explained in a letter home, little land in the

Preston area was under cultivation, but with the onset of the war, farmers were encouraged to cultivate as much land as possible. For every acre sown into oats, wheat or barley, the government guaranteed the farmer a payment of three pounds. The farmers were able to retain all the profit from their work, but were required to work under government supervision. For every acre of potatoes they sowed they received ten pounds. If they did not satisfy the expectations of the government, a supervisor would be appointed to directly supervise the farmer's work. These government incentives were established to increase the food supply so as to make Britain less dependent on imports.

It had been a most restful and enjoyable holiday with Reg and Popeye, much different from the leaves I had already had in Britain. I left hoping that I would see them again, but I never did. Having missed the train to Manchester where I would have changed trains for Nottingham, I had no choice but to try hitchhiking. I succeeded and arrived in Nottingham in time to contact Kay, a girl I had met at the Palais, and invite her to a movie.

I went back to Syerston the next day, to prepare once more to take to the air and to risk our lives in the hope that what we were doing would bring victory to the Allies sooner rather than later. It wasn't long before we were in "M for Mother" with a load of bombs to drop on harbour facilities at St. Nazaire on the French coast. The op was reported a success–only one aircraft was lost. However, on our return we were diverted to Ayre in Scotland because our airfield was fogged in.

Terry Goodwin

The following day, while returning to base, Terry turned the controls over to me while he climbed back to get an idea what could be seen from the astrodome. It probably was a foolhardy decision on his part to put me in the pilot's seat. I was so occupied in keeping the aircraft straight and level that a few seconds had passed before I was aware that the warning sound in my earphones was coming from the balloon barrage over Sheffield. We were heading right into it. Terry pulled me out of his seat, grabbed the controls and, with a sharp turn, avoided the barrage. Not surprisingly, Terry never let me behind the controls again.

In rapid succession, we took part in raids over Duisberg in the Ruhr Valley, then two raids over Berlin, and finally a raid to Essen, also in the Ruhr Valley, which was my last raid with 61 Squadron. Of all these raids, only the last was considered successful. Duisberg was completely cloud covered. The results of both the Berlin raids were disappointing, largely due to unfavourable weather conditions, poor marking of the various targets and failure of many of the bombs to explode. Losses were high, 2.3% on the first raid and 6.4% on the last.

On our return from the last raid, the shutdown of our port outer engine due to mechanical failure did not seriously affect the overall performance of our aircraft, since its bomb load had been dropped on what we hoped had been the target allotted to us. The day after our return from the first Berlin raid, we and other aircrews who took part in the raid were interviewed by reporters from several American and British papers. The following is a report that subsequently appeared in an American paper.

> **Great Splashes of Flames in Berlin Described by Wyncote Flier**
>
> *The raid was like Dropping a Tremendous Brick into a Huge Vat of Water, RAF man says.* Bombs over Berlin were like this to Sergeant Pilot Terry Goodwin, 22, of 168 Fernbrook Road, Wyncote, US, who looked down out of a Royal Air force bomber Saturday night. "It was just as if you had dropped a tremendous brick into a tremendous vat of water causing great splashes. Only these were splashes of flame."
>
> It was Sergeant Pilot Goodwin's third trip over Berlin and, he said, one of the liveliest shows of his nearly two year's service with the RAF. . . . A dispatch from a bomber base in England said Goodwin, tall, blonde and mustached, is one of the most popular men of his station. Describing the raid, he said: "It was quite concentrated, lasting not more than forty minutes,

I'd say. I saw one terrific explosion. One of our 4,000-pounders must have dropped on a big gas holder or tank, because flames leaped at least 3,000 feet into the air."

Goodwin stated that the raiders had no trouble with night fighters, but met fairly heavy resistance from ground defences. He said: "The defenses on the north side of Berlin were turned against us. Searchlights got our ship in their beams several times, but didn't hold us."

The following excerpt is from a Toronto paper.

**W.O. John Patterson's Performance Termed "Super Navigation"**

*Young Airman Known As "A Quiet, Very Studious and All-round Boy."*

Among the many Canadians attached to Lancaster bombing squadrons that attacked Berlin on Saturday night, was W.O. John Patterson of Bobcaygeon, a 21-year old navigator who was highly praised for the manner in which he found targets in spite of heavy clouds. His performance was termed "super-navigation."

While this bombing raid on Berlin appeared spectacular from the air, it was not very effective. It was only by a fluke that a secret Luftwaffe stores depot was destroyed.

The last op of my tour was on April 3/4, 1943 to one of the most heavily defended cities in Germany–Essen in the Ruhr Valley. I was apprehensive waiting for takeoff; would we complete it safely? While the raid was successful, losses were very heavy–6.1%, with two additional crashes in England of returning aircraft. Three hundred and forty-eight aircraft participated in the raid. We saw five shot down.

While I was on 61 Squadron, I gave a lot of thought to my future in the RCAF. Should I request a return posting to Canada if and when I completed my tour? Some Canadian aircrew were posted back; would I be one of them? I decided that it would be best for me to complete my second tour before returning to Canada. I did not relish the thought of becoming accustomed to a safe life in Canada, only to be posted back to England or to another war zone, such as the Far East. I did not want my parents to have to go through the anguish of another goodbye to me. Consequently, I decided to complete my second tour as quickly as possible. Terry and I had decided we would try to fly together again and, accordingly, volunteered to continue flying with 61 Squadron.

Unfortunately, or more likely, fortunately, as later events would prove in our case, Bomber Command normally required aircrew to take a break of about six months between tours at a conversion or operational training unit. I did give some consideration to re-mustering to a pilot and went so far as to make a formal request and to undergo an eye test to ensure my vision met the requirements needed to undertake pilot training. While I did pass the eye test, my request for a transfer was ignored. I wasn't overly disappointed, although I did feel that I would have proven capable of flying aircraft. However, upon graduation from university in 1949, I did acquire a private pilot's licence after two week's training at the Toronto Island airport.

Just prior to completing my last op with 61 Squadron, I was pleased to learn that I was now a pilot officer and could move into the officers' mess at my convenience. I lost no time and soon found myself sharing a batman or rather a batwoman with another officer. It was a great experience as I say in my diary,

*. . . to wake up in the morning to find my buttons polished and my shoes shined.*

However, my stay in the Syerston officers' mess was short. On completion of my tour I was given seven days' leave and informed that after I returned I would be posted to Upper Heyford where I had taken operational training.

The day before I left camp to commence my leave, I stood on the edge of the runway with other officers and members of the squadron to wave my crew off. Their target was Kiel on the Baltic Sea. Would they return safely? They did and eventually completed their tour as I had done. We were lucky. Of the fifteen aircrew members who joined 61 Squadron with me nine months before, only five had survived.

What to do on my leave? Why not try London again? I did and I wrote the following impression of my short visit.

*Why do we, you may wonder, spend our leave in London when it is bombed sporadically by that indiscriminate weapon of Hitler's that*

*has been called the "doodlebug" or "buzz bomb." Well, I don't think I know why we really come here. Perhaps it is because we can meet Canadian CWACs, WRENs or WAAFs. I hardly think that is the answer; they do not differ greatly from English girls. Perhaps some of us visit London only for the sake of being able to say after the war, when we return to Canada, that we visited the heart of the Empire, or maybe we visit London because we are curious about life under the continual threat of the doodlebug. Anyway whatever the reason, I am in London.*

*I read on a small screen, as I hand my ticket to the ticket collector at the platform barrier, the words "all clear." People hardly seem to notice. What difference does it make? They have to carry on whether the sign reads "all clear" or "alert." Riding down the escalator into the maze of London's underground, I begin to feel gushes of warm stale air that is full of dust churned up by swiftly moving wheels. On the platform people are trying to obtain some sleep. Impossible, I would say, especially those unfortunate ones who arrive too late to make their beds on one of the many two-tier cots that line the side of the tube. They can only sleep on the bare concrete floor, within two feet of the edge of the platform. I have to tread carefully or I will tramp on someone's toes. At first glance I am not favourably impressed by the people I see there . . . old people in dirty unkempt clothes, children with grubby faces and rough manners–but then it dawns on me that I, under similar circumstances, would probably look no better than they did. It is a shame that people must spend their nights in this way. What an environment for children. Will these children grow up to fit reasonably well into society or will they have a decidedly different outlook from children who are brought up in normal surroundings? How can they be healthy in this dust and heat, sleeping in filthy blankets and on dirty pillows? My heart goes out to them. Fate would have been kinder had they not seen this cruel unkind world. Coming down into the tube, I had overtaken an elderly lady singing in a shrill voice. She was intoxicated. Under one arm she carried a bundle of bedclothes and in the crook of the other, a small child. The poor boy turned his head and looked at us with puzzled eyes. "What is this all about?" they seemed to question.*

*The girls at the club had reserved a room for me. After seeing so many people sleeping or trying to sleep in the tubes, I was a bit doubtful as to whether I would sleep very well. I didn't. I believe I heard every air raid warning that night. I heard many explosions. Maybe most of them were imagined, but they kept me awake.*

*On the streets next day buildings that were up on my last leave were only rubble. A few streets here and there were barred by the words "keep out" or "closed to traffic." Very few people showed signs of lack of sleep. Only one person I remember hearing complain–a waitress in a restaurant. I heard her say she'd had only a few hours sleep in the last three days. Some people in London take every precaution even if it means going without sleep, but others take the view that if their time is up, there is nothing they can do about it and so spend their nights as they always did, above ground.*

*Hyde Park was full of people out to get fresh air and a little sunshine. Young couples, as they do in every country, especially in countries at war, were spooning on the grass. Children were playing beside the Serpentine under the watchful eyes of their parents; people were queuing to rent rowboats and on the other side of the pond, I could see youngsters diving and swimming.*

*London carries on as she always has done. Not even the doodlebug, Hitler's terror weapon, has succeeded in significantly interrupting London's war effort. The bug whizzes across the sky over the Straits of Dover, through the cloud and sunshine over the tops of farms, over the green quiet fields of England and through the industrial haze of London. Over the metropolis, its engine cuts; the bug has become a bomb. People scatter, some taking what shelter they can find; others lie on the ground waiting to hear the bomb explode. Afterwards, they get up, shake the dust off their clothes and continue on their way, seemingly unperturbed.*

I cut my stay in London short because I was concerned about my officer's uniform, which I had still not been able to claim from the tailors. Imagine having a made-to-measure uniform. It was a thrill I had never experienced before. My dress clothes on the farm had always been hand-me-downs from my father or one of my uncles. I was also anxious to learn if Terry and I were going to be given permission to complete our second tour with 61 Squadron without taking a six-month break between tours.

Upon my return and a visit to Tip Top Tailors in Nottingham, I was pleased to find a pilot officer's uniform, a greatcoat and raincoat waiting for me. I was now an officer, not only on paper but in uniform. However, while Bomber Command had first agreed to allow Terry and me to start our second tour without an intervening break, at the last minute the air officer commanding said "no dice." With the clarity of hindsight, considering the losses Lancaster squadrons were experiencing at that time, it was extremely unlikely that we would have survived a second tour.

While waiting for my posting, I volunteered to fly several times, once to collect meteorological data and other times to join bombing and air firing practice flights.

During this period the squadron lost one of its most experienced crews on a raid to Stuttgart on April 14/15, 1943. Twenty-two other aircraft were lost on this raid. Another one of our crews on a raid to Speza, an Italian port, were forced to ditch their aircraft on the sea on their return. While I don't know the full account of their ordeal, I know they were rescued from their dinghy three days later and returned to Syerston to resume flying.

Besides flying and hanging around the flight offices waiting for my posting, I visited Nottingham a number of times, looking up the girls I had met over the previous months. I realized it would probably be the last time I would see them and I did want them to know that I had enjoyed their company. They, with their smiles and their hugs, had helped me get through my tour. These girls gave me and other aircrew hope that we would some day have someone like them as our wives. I would miss them. I would meet other girls later, but I would never forget the girls I met at the Palais de Dance in Nottingham, especially Isobel. If circumstances had been a bit different, I might well have married her. As it was, while we corresponded for some time after I returned to Canada, she and I eventually went our separate ways.

# CHAPTER 9

## *Return to Upper Heyford as a Screen Navigator*

At last the posting came through. As the adjutant had told me some time before, I was being posted to an operational training unit at Upper Heyford, where I had taken my operational training. In a letter home I had this to say:

*While on this six-month rest period, I intend to take a course in journalism, learn to type and how to read and write the German language. This may not be possible but I will give it a try.*

Well, it was not possible. However, I did buy a second-hand portable typewriter, and eventually I did learn to type reasonably well, but not during that six-month period. As noted in another letter home:

*My posting finally came through and I am back at my former station where I spent some months last year. I am getting along well at my new job. I am a screen navigator so have not much lecturing to do. So far I have given only one short lecture and that was to some RAF cadets. We get one day off a week. Our leave does not come so often but that does not worry me, as I never know what to do with my leaves. My day off is Wednesday. I went into town [Oxford] Tuesday evening and stayed all the following day. I attended the dance and was glad to meet some of the girls I had met before.*

As a screen navigator, I was responsible for checking the navigational abilities of three to five navigators undergoing operational training by marking each navigator's log after he had completed a flying exercise. Occasionally, if I had doubts about a navigator's capabilities, I would fly with him. On one occasion, I had to recommend to the chief navigation officer that a navigator should be taken off the course. I was sorry to do this because I felt he was trying his best.

We did a lot of flying, although the flights usually were of short duration–two to three hours. The two-engine Wellington aircraft was a far cry from the Lancasters. Occasionally, trainee crews with an experienced pilot would, as part of their training, be required to drop leaflets over France at night. While the risk was not very great, some aircraft from Upper Heyford did experience anti-aircraft fire. Not all of the problems were caused by the enemy, however. On one leaflet raid, one of our aircraft was accidentally damaged by one of our own gunners, while he was testing his guns. Obviously, he had not noticed the other aircraft. In any case, the damaged airplane had to return to base. Unfortunately due to the damage, a safe landing was not possible so the crew bailed out. They all survived, but understandably were most upset to have been shot at by one of our own aircraft.

Of course, considering the amount of flying out of Upper Heyford, mostly by trainee crews at night, it was not surprising that there were several fatal crashes. One of my friends, a navigator, who like me had completed a tour of operations, was killed. He was older than I and had a small family in Nova Scotia. I expressed my condolences in a letter to his wife. She replied, thanking me for my letter and expressing the hope that I would survive. Over the years I occasionally wondered how she had coped with the death of her husband, a wonderful guy. While loss of life was much higher on 61 Squadron, I found that fatalities at Upper Heyford had a more profound effect on me. Perhaps it was because there were fewer of them, or we did not expect them, or because we had more opportunities to get to know one another better.

My letters home sometimes contained accounts of my observations on life in Britain. One such account taken from my letter dated May 13 follows:

*A sharp impatient rap breaks into my slumbers. I blink my eyes; seconds pass before I remember I am in Oxford. I answer the landlady's knock; she comes in to roll up the blackout saying, "Did you hear the news?" "No," I answered. (How could I? I was asleep.) "Churchill's in America." Common folk in Britain think a lot of their prime minister, but then, why shouldn't they?*

*A surprise awaits me, an egg for breakfast. I remember back in Canada how I used to become fed up with eggs. Now I am willing to go to great lengths just for one egg. What's in the cards today? A bit of shopping, then an aimless walk. Oxford, the city of higher learning;*

*where are the students and their professors? You don't meet them on the streets in the morning, only ordinary folk who seem no different from those of other cities except perhaps they are a bit more reserved.*

*The streets are crowded with shoppers and idle window gazers, elderly ladies, young ladies and their children, a few old men, including those toothless tobacco-chewing types, one or two national fire servicemen, a few air raid wardens whose duty it is to scan the sky for enemy bombers; and even a clergyman dressed in his long black robe, his head covered by a stiff wide-brimmed hat. Oxford's beauty has not been pockmarked by bomb craters. The colleges, slowly greying with age, continue to instill knowledge in the youth of Britain as they have done for hundreds of years.*

*The town hall clock strikes twelve and, I am reminded, a restaurant must be found if I wish to avoid queuing. Oxford, unlike most English cities, seems to abound with respectable restaurants if you know where to look for them, hidden away on second floors. Restaurants in England are much different from the restaurants I am familiar with in Canada, but then it should be remembered that I cannot, by any stretch of the imagination, be considered a connoisseur of Canadian restaurants. You walk in, decide the dining rooms are on the second floor and when you reach the restaurant area, you contemplate a minute or two before you finally walk into the one with the fewest customers. Like all restaurants in England, you wait patiently for every course. This gives you time to digest the first course before you tackle the next. After you finish the meal, you feel like beginning all over again. You never should be in rush. You must allow at least one hour for your lunch.*

*My fellow diners comprise a cross-section of people you would expect to find in a dining room in Oxford. Some distance from my table, there is a old man, possibly a retired professor with his wife, who reminds me of Mr. Chips in the movie Good-bye Mr. Chips. Near the window, a Norwegian airman is absorbed in what seems to be a pressing conversation with a girlfriend. The greater number of diners are middle-aged women, who like the professor's wife would rather eat this scanty meal than cook one of their own. They obviously do not have hearty appetites. One small dish of watery tasteless soup, two tiny slices of roast lamb, a bit of potato salad and a speck of apple sponge pudding without the apple, all for the amazing price of three shillings, with a glass of water if requested. After having to wait ten minutes for my bill, I left. At other places, you may have to wait up to half an hour.*

*Now for that walk in the esteemed city of Oxford, the city in which you can obtain one of the best educations in the world, if you can afford the tuition fees. A city that educates those with wealth while those without must be content with the education they can obtain in council schools, the schools that the more fortunate seem to think are good enough for ordinary folk, yet they themselves will not use them. Why educate the lower classes? That would mean some might gain high positions in life normally expected to go to the higher classes.*

*Oxford, with its streets bridged by trees, is a beautiful city. It is clean, so different in that respect to industrial towns of England. The homes are attractive with their healthy green hedges and tulips in bloom on their front lawns. There probably are slums in Oxford (the old poorly dressed men I have seen do not live in mansions), but they cannot be very extensive, as I have not seen any. Three o'clock finds me at the corner of Gypsy Lane and Shotover Road. Three Americans have just passed on horseback. None of them probably ever rode a horse before. A number of road workers stopped to stare at the riders. The horses appeared to be masters of the situation going wherever they thought the grass looked greener, crossing the road and almost giving some unlucky motorist heart failure.*

*They had disappeared around the corner and now two elderly, respectable-looking gentlemen have come, it seems, to join me on my bench. They have passed the best part of their lives and now only want to sit and chat about small seemingly unimportant matters, their dogs, the local news and their families. They have left and again even two older gentlemen come upon the scene. The old men of this area must have a monopoly on this bench. One has a full beard and, I gather by their clothes, they are not nearly as well off financially as the other two gentlemen; but by listening to their conversation, I gather they are just as happy. During middle age, wealth means a lot, but to the old it has no glitter. All they ask from life is peace and the necessities of life.*

May 14, it's my birthday.

*What does an airman do on his birthday at an air force base? Why not celebrate it in the usual RAF manner? Drink until your cares are swept away, until you only think of the present. A dangerous decision, but an exciting one.*

*Westwell and I are on a binge tonight. And who could think of a better reason than my birthday? We are the pub crawlers Churchill once mentioned. From pub to pub we stagger. A game of darts at the first, talk of our old squadron at the second and, at the last, we look for new interests–at the slim young lady standing at the bar sipping gin and tonic and bestowing coy glances at inebriated admirers. We drink until our better senses leave us and to our wavering eyes every one of these habitual pub-crawling women appear more attractive as time passes.*

*"Time is up ladies and gentlemen," the bartender shouts. It's ten; the pub closes and we push our way to the door with one of the notorious women of Fritwell. Fritwell Cora, they call her. [She wasn't really notorious; she was one of the few attractive young ladies in Fritwell. She stood out because Fritwell was such a small village that, if I remember correctly, could support only one pub–the Wheat Sheaf. Cora had a friendly smile for airmen and there were a lot of them staying at the Manor in the village centre, which was used to house airmen when there was no room in the main camp. Cora, like other young ladies, helped us to cope with life at Upper Heyford.]*

*We weave our way to the sweatbox, a tiny box-shaped dance hall so called because its poor ventilation makes you perspire as you never have before. We soon become accustomed to the repulsive smell of sweating human beings as we dance to the three-man orchestra. The perspiration dribbles down our faces, but we do not notice. We dance in oblivion to such petty discomforts. We are in a different world, it seems, forgetting our responsibilities as airmen–and that we may be behaving in a way we will regret tomorrow.*

*It's twelve now. The dance has ended. Westwell and I shove our way through the door jammed with other inebriates. We are beginning to sober up a bit. My conscience once more is beginning to make its presence known. Was it worth it? No, not in my view. People who drink a lot are weak. They have not the courage to face the world with . . . its never-ending problems, but prefer to obtain a false sense of seclusion from the past, present and future under the influence of alcohol.*

Having a break at the Wheat Sheaf Pub in Fritwell

Life went on at Upper Heyford. Our workload varied, depending on the number of crews on operational training. We continued our work as screen navigators and, at least once a week, sometimes twice, we would be required to spend the night in the control tower ready to assist in any emergencies. It was on one of these nights, when I had nothing to do but to wait for aircraft to return from a training exercise, that I put pen to paper.

*The sun moves down through the streaked sky growing redder as it slowly passes behind the smoky haze. The stars grow bolder and begin to wink and blink in the earth's great dome. A Hercules motor spits and stutters before it roars into life, its rough rhythm shattering the evening's silence like a splash ruffling the water on a still lake. The curtain rises, the first scene begins. More motors join the chorus–the whole aerodrome is alive–evening has passed and the night has come to an OTU. Aircraft taxi to the runway; the throttles are pushed open by the firm steady hand of the student pilot; the aircraft unleashed thunders down the runway like an angry bull. The plane rises, its glimmering lights rapidly gliding through the sky. One after another, with a two-minute interval, the aircraft take off, their lights growing fainter as they speed away on the first leg of the X-country. The curtain falls on the first scene. The audience is in suspense.*

*Will these new crews be worthy to follow in the vapour trails of their intrepid predecessors? The first glimmer of daylight is seen in the east; the stars lose their glitter and begin to fade in the early morning as the sun slowly starts another journey across the cloud-ribboned sky. The faint, tired drone of engines is heard; the aircraft are coming home. The curtain is lifted and Scene Two begins. The audience stirs from its reveries as they watch each pilot skilfully bring in his aircraft. They have all returned. Scene Two ends as the crews climb into their beds, quickly falling asleep, too tired even to dream.*

Occasionally, we were requested to undertake special flights, such as air/sea rescue or special visits to other airfields. Unfortunately, the rescue flights were never successful. Only once over the North Sea did we spot any human activity–a Norwegian fishing boat. These search missions took from five to seven hours of flying time. Nonetheless, they helped maintain our morale because one day we, ourselves, might be in the drink looking for help from our comrades.

Shortly after I had returned to Upper Heyford, Terry appeared. He undertook a special instructor's course at Upper Heyford while waiting to begin his second tour. Eventually he was posted to Barford, our satellite station. Consequently, we were able meet occasionally to discuss flying together on a second tour. Our desire now was to fly in Mosquitoes, the most versatile aircraft in the RAF, and possibly in all the Allied air forces. Both of us approached senior officers at our respective stations and also at Bomber Command for support.

Life was a lot different at Upper Heyford than it had been at Syerston. The work was more routine, although it was a far cry from an office job on civvie street. But we did get regular days off, which made up for the long periods between leaves. Some idea of how we passed our time as screen navigators can be gathered from this account I wrote:

**A Day at Upper Heyford, OTU**

My eyes are dazzled as I slowly open them. "Good morning," I mutter, turning over lazily. "It's seven-twenty," says the WAAF pulling back the blackout curtains to let in the fresh clean light of the sun's long rays. A new day has begun. Who cares? What an ungodly hour to rouse anyone. Not really, but to me who had gotten to bed late, it was. I roll over. The time quickly passes. Perhaps it is the footsteps in the corridor or perhaps it is my conscience that finally awakens me from my stupor. Eight fifteen, fifteen minutes to get breakfast. I hurriedly dress, taking just enough time to wet my face and run a comb through my hair.

Breakfast–porridge and sausage as usual. If it isn't sausage, it's bacon with fried tomatoes. But why complain. At least we have food. Nine o'clock finds me hastening to the flights with another day's work in the offing. A huge pile of navigators' logs awaits me. Will I ever get through my share? I begin to work, using my red marking pencil generously as I complain of this airman's mistake and that airman's lapse. I work through the morning almost as if I were flying with the aspiring Bomber Command navigators, murmuring approval when I find a well calculated wind, groaning when I encounter some huge blunder. Now how in the hell did this fellow get over here? Oh! He added the variation to his course incorrectly. Can't these navigators add? And so the morning passes. Twelve o'clock finally arrives and it's time to knock off.

Lunch! The soup is tasteless, the fish is good, but then who likes fish every third or fourth day? The dessert saves my life–chocolate pudding, one of my favourites. I help myself to a tiny cup of coffee and leave the dining room to sip it while I hopefully scan the mail rack for a letter from Canada. No such luck, no parcel either. Oh well, maybe I'll find some mail waiting for me tomorrow.

Daily Routine Orders (DROs) come next. Have they finally caught up with me? No, they haven't. No extra duties for another week. A newspaper is my next objective. Has the RAF ended the war yet? No such miracle has occurred. Ah! There's the *Daily Mirror*. Jane has not found her clothes. What a smutty mind that cartoonist must have.

One-thirty. It's time to return to the flights. More logs and still more of them. I begin to see red as I continuously use my marking pencil. What kind of school did this guy attend anyhow? He can't even add. The afternoon soon passes. It is five-twenty. Student navigators have been in for advice; others have just come in to comment about some insignificant problem.

The pile of uncorrected logs does not seem to have diminished. Will we ever be able to keep up to the never-ending flow of uncorrected logs? Perhaps the weather will clamp down. It does look like rain.

A cup of tea and a lettuce sandwich before I sink down into an easy chair to relax for fifteen minutes. An hour and a half until dinner. I spend it reading or doing algebra. One exercise in algebra a day is my target. I'll need more than a passing grade in algebra if I am going to university on my return to Canada. Seven o'clock is my shaving time. It may seem odd to some, but why shave in the morning when you have only to shave again should you want to go out in the evening? The dinner is an improvement over the luncheon, but whoever heard of asparagus on toast for dessert? It's eight o'clock now. The anteroom is almost empty. Most of the chaps have gone to the ENSA [Entertainment of the National Service Association] concert. I would have gone, but it was too late to obtain a ticket. I decide to sit in a comfortable chair to read the news more thoroughly and any of the editorials that interest me. The music from the force's radio program slowly trickles into my mind and the printed words begin to fade. I sit and stare, idly dreaming of Canada and my boyhood days. I sit this way, hardly moving, only glancing up when the telephone operator calls for one my fellow officers.

I go on dreaming until the chimes of Big Ben gently begin to bring me back to reality. I am in an air force mess in England. The acrid smell of dust and sweat disappears from my nostrils. I am no longer riding my favourite pony on the Saskatchewan plains. We are breaking up the Axis in Italy. Soon this war will be won and I will really be able to ride to the top of a hill and see the wide expanses of yellow sun-dried fields of the Canadian West, the only country I will ever call home.

My letters home continue to describe life as I found it at Upper Heyford. I also did my best to reply to my father's questions about the war and the progress being made to end it with an Allied victory. Here is how I commenced my letter of May 28:

*What a day outside! All my windows that overlook the entrance of our mess are open to obtain as much of the warm fresh air as possible. I can almost reach pink and red poppies. And the other flowers with their colours–blue, red, indigo, pink and purple–are a joy to see.*

In another I described a bike ride in the country with a friend:

*I've reserved this evening for you, no one else, just you folks at home. What are we going to do? Go for a cycle, of course. Remember, you will be coming with me. You will puff and perspire when I do. You will walk up the steep hills with me. It's seven forty-five p.m. We have had our dinner and a good dinner it was. Even the fish tasted better than it usually does; and so with a full stomach we begin our X-country. Where are we going? Nowhere in particular–we will cycle where fancy leads us.*

*A village comes into view at the bottom of a hill. We glide through past young girls swinging small cans, presumably selling tickets for a charity. Dirty-faced urchins raise their heads and stare at us momentarily before they go back to playing in the lush green grass at the side of the road. Our trusty steeds soon take us out of the village and we are in the quiet of the countryside. Nature's orchestra plays incessantly, the birds twittering, sheep baying, and in the distance a young calf bawling for its mother.*

*On our left a baling machine rests beside an old haystack, a bale still in the machine as if the workingmen had been hurriedly called away. We pass whole families out on the road for an evening walk. The smell of new-mown hay seeps into our nostrils. What an evening to be cycling! Cattle and sheep munching grass so contentedly. Is there a war on? Or have we been dreaming? The hum of three aircraft flying in practice formation is the answer. A hundred miles as the crow flies and this peaceful and calm evening will change into the hellish death-threatening sounds of war. The sounds of the aircraft leave us as we descend into another village. We are through it before we've had time to realize we were in one. We swerve around a bend to suddenly come upon a tiny bridge over a narrow canal not much bigger than the creek that flowed past our farm. We rest on the bridge with the village with its old thatched cottages slightly above and behind us. In front to our left and right there are two marshy fields of pastureland upon which sheep are grazing. Children are playing around a concrete blockhouse at the foot of the bridge erected when the lives of the British were dominated by thoughts of an imminent invasion.*

*We're on our way again. We meet a home guard on his bike, probably on his way to an evening of drill. We come upon a hill and now, as in life, we must work for the enjoyment we have experienced so far. The going finally becomes too steep and we walk. On our left we notice a large rectangular building. A small stream of water flows beneath it. It's an old mill. On the other side we see the race and the millpond held back by a dam near the side of the mill. We slowly push our bikes over the crest of the hill and once again we put foot to pedal. The shade of the umbrella of trees overhead soon cools us as we roll along, paying particular attention to nothing, forgetting our troubles; just letting nature soak in.*

*Another village comes into view and we pass two old men leaning over a hedge earnestly discussing some important issue (probably the quality of the beer being sold in the local pub). This village is no larger than the others. Soon we come upon a farmer and presumably members of his family hoeing the soil between rows of vegetables. Carrots as well as onions are well on their way to maturity. Farmers here seem to work as late as they do in Canada.*

*Finally, after another arduous climb from the river, we reach the main road. From now on the going will probably be downhill. To my surprise there are signposts on the road. I thought they had been taken down during the invasion threat. A lorry meets us, the only one we are likely to encounter on our cycle. The question of signposts is brought up again when we notice three about a half-mile apart, all bearing the same name and pointing in different directions. I would hate to depend on them to find my way. We hear a shot in the distance. Crows caw and circle a tree. Below it I see two men presumably testing their marksmanship on crows. A sporty looking car is in the gateway of the field. I wonder how they managed to get petrol to go shooting crows.*

*Our first three legs of our X-country tour have been completed and we decide to turn down an inviting path. Down hill our cycles take us through yet another village almost completely hidden in the green foliage of trees. We wonder if we will be able to speed safely around a corner looming ahead. We lean over to one side hoping our bikes will not skid out from under us. We make it, and almost without any effort on our part we are in another village. This jumble of small cottages, old and new, is blessed with a railway station, and for that reason the village is slightly bigger than the others. We pass two girls, one whom we overhear saying, "I wondered how long he was going to hold my hand." Obviously they were discussing their problems with young men. A few WAAFs and airmen walking beside the road remind us that we are almost home. Another mile and we arrive in the first village we passed through. It is Wings for Victory Week. Two young boys sell us raffle tickets for a pet rabbit.*

*An RAF lorry with a trailer parked beside the village pub is drawing a lot of interest from the villagers. It is loaded with RAF paraphernalia and presumably has been visiting villages in connection with the Wings for Victory Week. An RCAF officer asks me what the large drum is on the trailer. A 4,000-pound bomb, I tell him, but not a real bomb–a replica of one. It was lucky he asked, because had someone in the crowd asked him, he, an air force officer, would have been embarrassed not knowing what some of the bombs looked like that the RAF was dropping over Germany. We leave the crowd to gape with wonder at the bomb and in a short while we are back at the officers' mess.*

Life went on. Well, not for everyone. There were two crashes. No reason was given for the first one, possibly because its cause could not be determined with certainty. All the crewmembers perished, yet all members of the crew of the second crash survived. The bomb-aimer had mistakenly closed the cock on the fuel line feeding the engines.

It was about this time that McCelland, who had been with me at Syerston, and I learned that we had been awarded the Distinguished Flying Cross (DFC). My award was not for any particular act of bravery, but probably because of the life-threatening hazards I faced many times on bombing raids. In my view it also recognized the loss of my fellow airmen, who had not survived the risks we all took.

In the officers' mess, we would often talk of the war and the progress being made to bring victory to the Allies. There was a lot of discussion concerning a second front. When would it take place and where? Most of us thought sooner rather than later. As stated in my diary, I forecast attacks would take place simultaneously through the Balkans and on the French coast.

My father in a letter stated he could not understand how Germany could withstand the terrific bombardment it was receiving from the Allied air forces. In my reply, dated June 21, 1943, I stated:

*Think of Coventry and you will have an answer to your question. Do you think Britain would have asked for peace if Coventry, London and other cities had been bombed more often than they were and with a greater weight of bombs? No, Coventry could have been razed to ground level, the derelict of every building a grim reminder of the past, but Britain would never have admitted defeat. It is true the residents of Coventry might have been ready to call it a day but what chance would their voice have had against the residents in the many other cities in Britain hardly touched by bombs. So it is in Germany. We have defeated the residents of the Ruhr [Valley] but we certainly have not made much headway with the remainder of Germany. Until we can bomb every large city in Germany with devastating effect simultaneously–and when I say simultaneously, I mean within a few weeks of each other–we can never hope to win this war within the next twelve months by airpower alone. . . . We can bomb Germany systematically, one city after another as we are doing now. It [the bombing] is disrupting Germany's war efforts and the morale of the people is falling. But will that ever win the war? During the time we spend bombing several cities, another one has had time to rebuild its industries and to regain a sense of security. If we could keep up the bombardment year after year, it would probably bring the war to an end, but would our morale stand the strain? Can we go on fighting with no definite end in view? I leave you to reply to that question.*

Parcels kept coming from home. In several letters I informed my parents that the food was much better in the officers' quarters, and so special foods from home were no longer as welcome as when I was a non-commissioned officer. I now saved the food from home for relatives and other persons who I felt would appreciate it. In a letter home, I explained that I gave a box of the cheese to one of my friends for his wife who had just had a baby. At the "Wings for Victory" auction held in the officers' mess, a can of peaches I donated sold for twenty pounds.

Life at an OTU had other hazards besides those associated with flying. They were not nearly so serious, but could make living uncomfortable. The crab louse was one and I wasn't the only officer to have an itchy crotch. Three other screen navigators were making regular visits to the medical centre using various creams to poison the critters. We probably picked them up at one of the

Oxford boarding houses in which we stayed. I presume there may have been lice in the bedding. In any case, getting rid of the lice was not easy. The rash they produced was particularly troublesome when I rode my bike.

Another week's leave. I decided to spend part of it with my aunt and uncle in Liverpool and the remainder in Blackpool. Liverpool was not one of my favourite cities, but I had had an invitation for some time and I was looking forward to some home cooking. Fortunately, my cousin Nora would be home at the same time, so I could count on her to take me around the city. She did more than that. She introduced me to an attractive young lady whom I was able to take out on several occasions. I was impressed. Had she lived near or in Oxford, I would have, I am sure, tried to establish a close relationship. As it was, I never saw her again. Such was the life of an airman.

Blackpool was a disappointment. A friend I met there and I spent hours trying to locate a room, only to find a dingy, untidy one that was furnished with one bed hardly wide enough for two persons. The bathtub was filthy. I made the mistake of opening a cupboard to find it full of dirty clothes. Not surprisingly, early the next morning we looked for another room. After searching for two hours, we gave up and found ourselves at the station waiting for a train to Preston. While we did have an opportunity to walk along the beach for a short while and to visit the Fun Fair, I was not impressed. Possibly if we had visited at another time when the trains and town were not so crowded, and the weather had not been so hot and sultry, we would have been more favourably impressed.

As it was, we were glad to leave for Preston. Of course this industrial city could hardly be considered an improvement over Blackpool. However, at the first hotel we visited, we were able to rent a room. We only stayed in Preston overnight, as there was little to interest us. We did go to a dance but, like most dances in England during the war, it was soon over and we had nothing to do but to retire to our hotel room. On my way home I stopped in Liverpool for another short visit with my aunt and uncle. While there I took time out to purchase the secondhand typewriter upon which I planned to learn to type.

On my return to Upper Heyford, I was pleased to learn that I had won a seven-pound, ten-shilling savings certificate in a sweepstake, run in the officers' mess. Not very much, but enough to cover the cost of a couple of nights in Oxford. I was soon back in the navigation office working with the never-ending stream of navigators and bomb-aimers passing through Upper Heyford on their way to join a squadron. Little did they know what was in store for them. Nor did we go out of our way to inform them of the high casualty rate. However, we did do our best to ensure that they would be able to perform the tasks for which they would be responsible. Occasionally, we might suggest that a navigator be assigned the duties of a bomb-aimer and that a bomb-aimer be assigned the duties of a gunner. I did not relish having to turn in an unfavourable report but if I hadn't, I might have put the life of a crew in jeopardy.

I continued to have concerns about my immediate future in the RAF. Would I be posted on a second tour of operations at the end of six months as a screen navigator? If so, would I be posted to a Mosquito squadron with Terry as my pilot? If not, what about remustering to pilot? I pestered our wing commander on several occasions and I visited the Air Ministry in London to obtain an indication of what I could expect. It was all to no avail. I would just have to be patient. A decision would eventually be made.

So I carried on. There were two aircraft crashes in July, one due to engine failure and other to a collapse of a wing. Fortunately, only one life was lost. In our free time during the warmer weather, the small river that flowed nearby became a favourite recreational area. We went swimming often and occasionally I would go fishing with a farmer whom we had gotten to know in one of the local pubs. He and his wife became good friends of a number of us and occasionally I would visit them at teatime.

We, of course, continued to visit Oxford, not only to meet girls at the dances in the city hall but to take advantage of tours that were arranged for us from time to time. One day, an attractive university student took me on a tour of three colleges, including Christ Church. I had expected to see huge classrooms, but I did not see any. The only desks I saw I considered antiques, and they were covered with masses of carved initials. I noted there were no benches or chairs. While I was impressed by the architecture of the buildings, there was no central heating and the rooms were drafty and damp. My guide probably was not impressed with my lack of knowledge. I could not read the Latin inscriptions nor did I know the difference between Norman and more modern architecture. Still, she was very patient. She told me how students were taught in the colleges–there were few lectures. Students were on their own most of the time. They were given assignments, some reference material and then expected to prepare an essay during a given time period. Having only been subjected to high school classes, I had trouble picturing myself as a student in Oxford.

On July 29, 1943, in Oxford, I purchased a jacket and a pair of pants. In the summer heat, I found my uniform uncomfortable and so when out of camp I would often change into my jacket and flannels. It was not long before my friends learned what I was doing, so those who were about the same build as I would borrow the jacket and pants from time to time. Eventually, we may have worn them out or I may have given them to a friend when I was posted home. During hot weather, although I felt the uniform attracted the opposite sex, I was quite willing to forgo its élan for comfort.

Besides cycling, there were other activities we could pursue to relieve the pressures of our work. We played soccer occasionally and tried to interest our English friends in softball, but without much success. Fishing was also on our list of recreational activities, as noted in one letter home:

*Two of us had today off so decided to try our luck at fishing. My fishing partner is English so I let him do all the planning. I still had some honey and cheese left [from one of my parcels from home] so he had one the mess girls make us some sandwiches. When I woke up this morning, it was very misty; I rolled over and went back to sleep, thinking our outing would not take place. But at ten-thirty, Ron appeared. The weather had improved somewhat, but it still was not favourable. However, we decided to chance it. I am glad we did, because the weather turned out fine. We fished, slept on the grass, and swam in the canal. Except for the fact we did not catch any fish, everything went according to plan. On our way back we even managed to beg a glass of milk from a comely daughter of a local farmer.*

While we occasionally continued to attend dances in the Sweat Box, we were pleased one evening, because of the hot weather, to receive an invitation to attend a lawn dance.

*I did nothing, just sat on the grass watching the dancers unconsciously entertaining me. Children and young people formed the cast. A three-man orchestra provided the music: a rattling drum, a blaring saxophone and a groaning piano. It was amusing to see children dancing, some of them perhaps for the first time. A little girl was dragging her still younger boyfriend around. He did not seem to be overly interested. He doesn't know how lucky he is. Woe is man when women begin to attract his roving eyes. You could hear no shuffling or scraping; the grass was a quiet as a plush carpet. The boys and I just relaxed, content to watch the curious antics of human beings dancing. Westy went so far as to say it was the spontaneous expression of human emotion by physical motion.*

Back at base, life went on, but not for everyone. There were two more aircraft crashes in which nine crewmembers lost their lives. Considering that Upper Heyford was a training establishment, we appeared to be having an abnormal number of crashes. I don't recall the underlying reasons for these and some other crashes, possibly because I was not informed.

On a day off, I cycled to Barford to visit Terry. He was confident that at the end of our six-month break we would be going back on ops together. Another leave began for me on August 20. I had decided to spend most of it in London, where I planned to meet Wallace Martin, a friend from Bobcaygeon, who was also in the RCAF. During the visit, he and I were fully occupied touring the city. We visited St. Paul's Cathedral, the Tower Bridge, St. James Park, Buckingham Palace, the Tower of London and Westminister Abbey, where we attended a church service.

On returning to Upper Heyford, I had this say about the progress of the war:

*We still have a long way to go, but things look brighter now that Denmark has revolted against the Nazi regime. Berlin is being softened up and Russia continues to be successful in its offensive. So for the time being, I see no reason why we cannot be confident that the future holds large prizes for the Allies.*

Reading my diary covering the remainder of the year, I note that our OTU lost four more aircraft: September 4–engine failure. Crew bailed out safely. September 28–two aircraft crash in mid-air. Only one survivor out of twelve crewmembers–one of the pilots. December 13–reason for the crash not recorded, all crewmembers killed. Not surprisingly, following a crash aircrew morale would decline, but not for long. We would soon return to normal if you can call living on an air force station as normal. Far from it. There was always something going on–well, nearly always. We spent a lot of time wishing the war would end so that we could start a normal life.

Terry and I continued to badger our senior officers at our respective airfields to determine when we would be posted to a squadron. On September 30, 1943, our W/C informed me that no Canadians were to be posted back on operations. Did this signal the end of our efforts to return to operations? Could we now expect to be posted back to Canada? There were no answers, not for me anyway. I did not want to be a screen navigator for the remainder of the war nor did I want to be an instructor in Canada. I wanted to get on with my life. Let's get the war over, was my feeling, so I could go home for good and not have to face the possibility of returning to combat. Presumably, there may have been other Canadian airmen who felt as Terry and I did, because on October 23, the adjutant told me I could apply for a Mosquito posting if I signed a statement saying I did not want leave in Canada. I signed.

In the meantime, I continued with my work as a screen navigator. Of course there were several other activities for which I had responsibility, such as taking on the duties of the orderly officer, night air control officer or parade officer. Occasionally, I would be asked to talk to lower ranks on various subjects, some of my own choice.

*I spent a very enjoyable day off duty yesterday. A friend from our section and I went for a cycle to a neighbouring aerodrome about twenty miles away to see the pilot with whom he flew on operations. We found his flight office without any trouble. While there I met another pilot who had been attached to 61 Squadron. Both their wives lived nearby so they suggested that we have tea with them as they, themselves, could not get away until later. They were really nice people. I was surprised, as I sometimes find English people not as friendly as they could be. There was baby girl in one of the families, a cute kid who was very well behaved, considering she was a baby. I enjoyed playing with her. One of the families was staying in an old abandoned pub. The childless couple lived in a trailer, or caravan as they called it. The wife seemed quite proud of it and certainly did not complain that there was not better accommodation. It is very cozy–perhaps a bit too cozy; there is hardly room to stand up. The lady was very hospitable, more so than other ladies I had met in England. She gave us a glass of beer while we discussed her husband's life in the RAF. She did not have much to look forward to, living in a trailer until the war ended. You know I am impressed by the Brits, but I suppose under similar circumstances, Canadian people would carry on as best they could. When we left she offered to give us a snack and gave us a pressing invitation to come back again. We may do so sometime, although it is a long way to pedal a bike.*

It must have been hell for these two ladies and others like them living a short distance from the airfield from which their husbands took off on flights possibly never to return. In the evenings they would hear the aircraft take off knowing their husbands were on board and then, in early hours of morning, they would hear the aircraft overhead, wondering if heir husbands were among the aircrews who had returned.

Occasionally, we were sent to Barford, our satellite airfield, to take charge of the navigation office. As you will note in the comments made in my letter home on October 29, I was not at all impressed by our accommodation.

*My stay at the other camp was not very enjoyable. Perhaps I would have gotten to like it if I had stayed longer. It was too much like a lumber camp. Everyone sleeps in Nissen huts, the kind they use in Iceland. The first night I nearly froze to death; the second night I managed to find some wood to start my fire. I had a real one going in no time. I did manage to get my room warm, but as soon as the fire went out it began getting cold again. However, I had a good sleep that night. These Nissen huts have concrete floors. The walls and ceiling, which are curved in the shape of half a barrel, are made of galvanized iron. There is no insulation whatever. Parts of the floors are covered with linoleum; the remainder is just bare concrete. To top everything, the weather has been very cold and damp. Your clothes feel damp all the time.*

Back at Upper Heyford, on November 4, we were able to have our first fire of the fall in our room. If we were careful, our monthly coal ration provided enough for two fires a week. I did not think very much of our fireplace. It was not very efficient. You had to be almost over the fire to feel its heat. Fortunately, the main section of our mess was centrally heated so that if we felt cold in our room, we could grab a book and have a comfortable read in the anteroom. However, while I may have been cold on the evening of November 4, I was not cold two evenings later. That was the night we invited to our mess the dancers and actors from the musical production *The Magic Carpet*, which was a great hit with the Upper Heyford audience. Previous to the visit *The Magic Carpet* had been playing at the Princess Theatre in London. The female performers were beautiful, and chatting with them took away all thought of my cold room.

Another interesting leave experience: some time before, to taste the life of a sailor, I had made arrangements to join a destroyer flotilla. Unfortunately, the flotilla had not been informed of my intention. However, after staying in the Fountain Hotel in Sheerness overnight, arrangements were made for me to board the destroyer *Pycheley*. It was a great experience. The food was good and I enjoyed the company of the officers. I spent a lot of time on the bridge. It was rather cold, but I soon got accustomed to that. Perhaps it was the heavy underwear I had on. I was shown all over the destroyer and was free to go wherever I pleased. I was able to compare their navigational methods to ours and concluded that with the tools we had then, it was more difficult to navigate in the air.

Although the men were well fed, I felt they nonetheless had a hard life. While at sea, they were required to be on duty for four hours then off for four hours. Two of the officers did not even have bunks, but got what little sleep they could on the sofa in the wardroom, which they shared with me. On certain types of duty the men had to be on call at all times. That meant they would have to get what sleep they could at whatever post they were required to man on the destroyer. It was the weather that got them down. They had to spend so much time on deck, often getting wet, which added to their discomfort.

While steaming through the English Channel on our way to Portsmouth, I spent about seven hours at different times on the bridge with the skipper. He told me that there was not much chance of spotting any U-boats because the sea was too rough. While at sea, the skipper remained on duty at all times either on the bridge, or, when conditions permitted, in his sea cabin, a tiny hut just a step away from the bridge.

Shortly after docking in the Portsmouth harbour, we pulled up anchor and retraced our route to Sheerness. I was pleased that I had been given an opportunity to taste life at sea on a destroyer.

During my subsequent leave in London, I found myself in the company of some distinguished personages. At an officers' club I met Mrs. Massey, the wife of Canada's high commissioner, Vincent Massey, and two days later, after I had left the *Pycheley*, at a party at the Wings Club, I danced with a viscountess. Vic Oliver, a well-known comedian, and the husband of one of Churchill's daughters, and Irving Berlin, a popular American songwriter, were guests at this party. The following evening a friend and I were introduced to a Lady Forest, who in turn introduced us to two young ladies in the British armed forces who accepted our invitation to dinner. So, for a while, it appeared I was climbing the ladder of British society. It was just a taste but, nonetheless, it was exciting for a young man who two years before had been working for eight dollars a week as an electrician's helper.

November 21 found me on a train en route to Oxford, where I would catch a local train to Upper Heyford. That citizens of many countries were involved with the war effort in Britain was indicated by the people who were sharing the compartment with me. First there was the Frenchman who was returning with me to Upper Heyford. He had had an accident as a result of which one of his feet was in a cast. I had to assist him to board the train. Then there were two young ladies, a member of the US army, and a citizen of Greece. Britain was represented by an older woman. The two other passengers were young men, one from Australia and the other from Czechoslovakia. So seven nationalities were represented in the compartment.

On my return, I was back at work with a new course of navigators. Unfortunately, crashes still occurred. Two aircraft collided in mid-air, killing all but one on board, including two of our staff who, like me, had completed a tour of operations. We carried on as we always did, hoping that somehow or other we would be spared. Looking back, I marvel at why I kept trying to get back on operations. Why did I not sit back and let fate take over or was I taking the right approach? After all, if I did complete a second tour, it would have been very unlikely that I would be expected to do any more operational flying. Anyway, my recent promotion to flying officer meant a higher salary and more money to send home. Would I live to spend it?

Time passed without anything special taking place until December 30, when I was asked to take high altitude tests in a decompression chamber. My test concluded: "This officer was taken to the height of 37,000 feet on both tests, which were of two hours' duration. No pains or symptoms were in evidence at any time during the complete tests. FOUND FIT FOR HIGH ALTITUDE FLYING." So now that I had been judged fit, when would I be assigned to Mosquitoes? Would Terry and I be posted together? The adjutant said he would take steps to ensure we were. There was nothing we could do but wait for developments.

While this was going on, Westy surprised me by asking me to be his best man at his upcoming wedding. I hadn't known that he was seriously contemplating marriage, but then that was not surprising because he had known his prospective bride only for a short time. How could I refuse even if I had never attended a wedding? So after getting a special weekend pass, I took the train to the small community of Wimbourne, near Bournemouth, where the wedding was to take place. When I arrived at the bride's home, I found her family in a panic. The bride's mother was ill and last-minute arrangements had become the bride's responsibility. The bride's father did not know whether he was coming or going. He appeared to be in a state of shock, presumably because the courtship had been so short. Yet, the following day, the wedding ceremony took place without any obvious problems. The dinner, however, was the highlight of the day for me. In a letter home I said:

*We had a wonderful dinner at the reception. I ate and ate. I even managed to get two pieces of wedding cake. It had thick icing on it and did not seem to lack for fruit. The most delicious dish of all was the trifle, which had been amply flavoured with sherry. After the dinner, toasts were made, including mine to the bridesmaids.*

There was one problem, however. Westy and I had a drink or two prior to the ceremony and he may have drunk more wine at the dinner than he should have. Consequently, afterwards, when we were all walking into the village, Westy's behaviour was a bit out of line considering he was now the husband of an attractive lady. Actually she went so far as to tell him if he did not straighten up she would leave him then and there. He did get himself under control. In the 1960s while in London on business, I enjoyed a visit with Westy and was pleased to learn that he was still happily married to the lady who had threatened to leave him on their wedding day.

Christmas in the RAF: What was it like? For a description, let's read part of my letter home dated December 30,1943.

Allen Westwell's wedding

*Christmas has come and gone and I am none the worse for it. If you had been with us, you would have wondered how we could go back to work. On Christmas Eve, we had an all-ranks dance in the airmen's mess. Like all mess dances, it was a wild affair but I believe everyone enjoyed themselves. Christmas morning we were going to have an egg for breakfast so I got up for it but then went back to bed. As a consequence, I missed the comic football match in which the players put on comic costumes and played without any set rules. At noon fourteen other officers and myself served Christmas dinner in the airmen's mess. I was lucky. I was the bartender; all I had to do was serve beer. There was an ample supply and so no airman went away complaining about the bartender. The food was good.*

*After leaving the airmen's mess, we had an ordinary everyday lunch in our mess. Lunch over we attended a variety concert put on by ENSA. It was very good, at least according to my tastes. I was in fits of laughter. Our dinner at eight-thirty was a success, the best dinner I have had in England. We had turkey, duck and chicken. The Christmas pudding was really good, but I could have eaten more. The cake was not as tasty as those I have had in Canada, but I don't think the cook could be faulted. He just did not have enough fruit to put into it. Dinner over, we migrated to the airmen's mess, where the station ball was being held. It, just as wild as the other one, was obviously enjoyed by all the participants.*

*On the following day, Boxing Day, I went for a cycle to get some fresh air in my lungs. That over, I wrote a letter, then joined the boys in the anteroom for tea. The sergeants were having their dance tonight. It was not quite as wild as the others and there was a well-prepared buffet. While I enjoyed the dance, I went back to my room early because I wanted to be fit for work the following morning. That ended our Christmas celebrations, all except the stag party in the sergeants' mess. Few officers took advantage of the sergeants' invitation. They had had enough during the previous three nights.*

But then there still was the arrival of the new year to celebrate. Most of us showed up at the New Year's Eve dance, which like the other all-ranks' dance, was held in the airmen's mess and everyone seemed to have a good time. Although I think that in part could be attributed to the amount of alcohol consumed.

Still I did not have a particularly good time, due to a phone call I had made earlier to Terry. He informed that he was being posted to a

Christmas Day at Upper Heyford

Mosquito unit in the morning. I did talk to our adjutant and he promised to do what he could for me. I wasn't optimistic. After all our efforts to get back on ops together, we were not going to succeed.

The new year had arrived. What did it hold for me? Would I continue working as a screen navigator, would I soon be sitting beside a pilot in a Mosquito over Germany, or would I find myself on a troop ship returning to Canada? My activities at Upper Heyford continued without change, although they could hardly be classified as routine. Except when on leave, I never knew for certain what I would be doing the next day. However, one task that I could count on was the weekly lecture I gave to airmen over whom I had limited responsibility. These lectures covered a wide range of subjects, such as "The French People," "Armies of Occupation" and "Relations with America." I was given printed material to assist in my sessions but on one occasion I was given an opportunity to choose the topic. I chose "Farming in Saskatchewan." The session went well, possibly because I knew my subject first hand. There were lots of questions.

Looking back, I realize I was fortunate in having parents who were concerned about my welfare and my morale. The letters and parcels kept coming, sometimes taking four or five weeks to find me, but no matter, they were always welcome. Presumably in one of her letters my mother mentioned how fate played an important part in our lives. In reply I had this to say:

*Mother, you believe too much in fate. Just because someone does not do something he had planned to do does not mean that fate has stepped in and has taken an interest in his affairs. This believing in fate is a lot of poppycock. If you want anything in life, fate will not stand in your way. It's up to you, you yourself.*

My father in one of his letters wanted to know if I had any plans for the future. I replied:

*Well, you will agree it is very difficult to plan in wartime. However, one thing is fairly certain. I will be over here for about another year. By that time I believe I can count on having saved $3,500; or am I being too optimistic? What would be the best way to make use of this money? With it and the help of the government I could buy a reasonable farm but will farming conditions be any better than they were before the war? Suppose we forget about farming* *for the present, then how can I make use of this money? Perhaps I will be qualified to take a course at a university. Suppose I took an engineering course. That would take three or four years. I could take a course in journalism, possibly in one year. But is it worth it? Many men have worked their way up to well-paid and responsible positions. Do you think that opportunities of that kind may arise or do you think it would wiser to take a course? Unfortunately, under all this there is a woodpile with a monkey in it. Suppose I decide to get married someday. Then what happens?*

In the meantime, I continued to correct navigators' logs, fly occasionally, play squash or table tennis in the evenings, cycle in the countryside, or bus into Oxford to a dance–hopefully with a beautiful young lady–or to see the latest movie. But what I liked best of all was to visit my friend and his wife on their farm close to Fritwell. Sometimes Herb would take me with him in his truck to the agricultural market in Banbury. There I would talk to the farmers and learn a bit more about farming in England. At the same time I would tell them about the huge farms in Saskatchewan and the wide-open prairies. They may have had some difficulty in believing the stories I told them of large cattle ranches and branding time in the spring. On our return, Herb's wife, Doris, would have an appetizing supper ready; then, after Herb had done his regular evening chores, he and I would visit the Wheat Sheaf Pub, where we were almost certain to meet some of my colleagues from Upper Heyford.

Letter writing continued to occupy me for hours at a time. I was very touched at this time to receive a parcel from the Moshers in Halifax. Their son Paul, as I have already mentioned, was killed on an op over Germany in July 1942.

My screen navigator's responsibilities were rapidly ending. Soon I would be back on an operational squadron. Life at Upper Heyford had proven to have its ups and downs–up when enjoying a bike ride in the countryside, the company of attractive young ladies or a game of darts in the Wheat Sheaf Pub–down, when I felt obliged to state that an airman's performance was not satisfactory, or when aircraft crashes or other accidents took place accompanied by loss of life.

# CHAPTER 10

## *Life on a Pathfinder Squadron*

On the morning of January 17, 1944, I was feeling pretty good; not on Cloud Nine, but nonetheless enjoying a high, an uplifting of my spirits. My posting had come through! But then, a few hours later, it was cancelled with no explanation. There was no way now that I would be able to fly with Terry. Ten days later I was informed again that my posting had been approved. This time, it was final and in a few days, I was on my way to the Marham, near King's Lynn in Norfolk County where my pilot and I, whoever he turned out to be, would learn to fly and navigate a Mosquito. Guess whom I met in the officers' mess? Terry. Was there still a chance I would fly with him? No. Because of time limitations, he had had no choice but to crew up with another navigator, an officer who had served with us at Syerston. Terry was leaving to join his new squadron in a few days.

The following day, the squadron leader in charge of training interviewed me to determine what type of training I should take. Should I join the Mosquito squadron responsible for collecting meteorological data over Germany for use by Bomber Command; or should I join a pathfinder squadron? My choice was the Pathfinder Force, which had been formed in August 1942, to find and mark designated targets.

My choice was accepted and I soon began specialized training in the use of a target marking aid known as "Oboe." This blind bombing device, when installed in a high-flying aircraft, enabled operators in England to direct the aircraft to the target and signal the navigator when to release the target markers. Only one aircraft could be directed at a time and so to ensure that the target was marked at short intervals, Oboe was not activated by the marking aircraft until it was within eight to ten minutes' flying time of the release point. Hence, the navigator's main problem was to get his aircraft to the pre-arranged Oboe turning point very close to the pre-arranged time. The navigator would turn on the Oboe equipment and the pilot would start receiving dots or dashes from the "cat" station situated on the southeast coast of England if the aircraft was to the right or left of the bombing run; or a steady signal, if the aircraft was on the bombing run. It was the pilot's responsibility to maintain the aircraft on the bombing run and to maintain the altitude, usually between 30,000 and 32,000 feet, which had been given to him during briefing. All the navigator had to do, once Oboe was operating, was listen, with the bomb release in his hand, to signals originating from the mouse station situated on the east coast of East Anglia. These indicated to him when to release the markers. The bombing track progress signals received by the navigator prepared him to push the bomb release button exactly at the right moment. While Oboe did increase bombing accuracy, unfortunately its range was limited to no more than 350 miles from the cat and mouse transmitting stations.

Because the markers burned for a limited time, it was necessary to have backup pathfinder aircraft, usually Lancasters or Halifaxes, which, with flares, would keep the target marked for the main force bombers until another Mosquito dropped its marker about ten to fifteen minutes later. During the target-marking run, in order to ensure that the markers were dropped on the target or very close to it, the pilot had to maintain a straight and level flight at a constant altitude. Fortunately, we flew at an altitude rarely reached by flak, although on one occasion, shortly after joining our squadron, we were conned in searchlights for two minutes and felt the concussions of flak bursting below us.

I was posted to 109 Squadron, the only squadron besides Squadron 105 that was equipped with the Oboe device. My pilot was S/L Cobb, who was older than many of us and somewhat more reserved. Although I spent a lot of time with him, I never got to know him well. Of course, that was probably because of our age difference. I never asked him many questions about his personal life, and in the mess, not surprisingly, he tended to associate with the older officers. He never went to dances and he very rarely rode a bike. Of course, having a car probably accounted for that. We called him Cobby. It was the only name we had. If I ever knew his Christian name, I have long since forgotten it. However, Cobby and I got along well together as a crew. He was a good pilot and I presume he was satisfied with my navigational abilities.

There was a lot of training ahead of us. Cobby had to be checked out on the Mosquito and I had to sharpen my navigational skills and learn how to let Oboe take us down the bombing run. I attended many lectures, not all of which concerned navigation. For example, we learned about the damage inflicted on German targets by Bomber Command and aircrew escaping from prisoner-of-war camps in Germany. As at Upper Heyford, there were accidents, but they were not as frequent. In one aircraft crash, two members of our course were killed.

A Mosquito aircraft

Of course, we navigators did not spend all our time in lecture rooms or flying in training aircraft such as the Oxford, a small two engine plane that during the war was used to train thousands of aircrew throughout the Commonwealth. We cycled through the countryside, hoping to find a pub or a restaurant that could give us better food than we had in our mess. Sometimes we would succeed, but not often. We attended dances whenever we could but unfortunately they were a far cry from those in the Palais de Dance in Nottingham. Occasionally, McClelland, who had been with me at Upper Heyford and Syerston, would accompany me. Mac had arrived at Marham at about the same time as I had. He, too, was going to 109 Squadron and we saw quite a bit of each other. Little went on in our mess. Occasionally, we would play bridge or sing songs around the piano. Interest perked up a bit, though, when the Duke of Gloucester joined us for lunch one day. As noted in my diary, I was annoyed when I observed that the duke and the senior officers were served better food than we were. I surmised that was to be expected in a class-conscious country.

For reasons unknown to me, my mail from home took longer than it had previously taken. Possibly part of the problem was my posting from Upper Heyford. The mail sorters at the overseas delivery point must have had quite a time keeping track of armed force personnel.

*It will please you to know that your two Christmas parcels finally arrived [March 8]. There was also one from Rev. Howard of Bobcaygeon. Your parcels were intact. The sweets are OK; the boys certainly like them. I still have not received the parcel with the map in it. I suppose that one has gone to the bottom of the "drink."*

The comments I made on the American air force in the same letter indicate that we were well aware of the important role they were playing in trying to convince the Germans of the futility of prolonging the war.

*Well, what do you think of the American air force now? They are putting on a wonderful show, don't you think? They will soon be showing us up. Attacking Berlin in daylight and not losing many more aircraft than us. I admire them for their intestinal fortitude and for the short time it took them to put as many aircraft in the air as we have. We, a whole empire, let one country surpass us in aircraft production. Whatever her shortcomings, she is doing her full share and a bit more. I only hope that she will continue to do her full share after the war towards maintaining a permanent peace.*

I will leave you, the reader, to decide whether the United States has, in fact, continued to do its share.

All our letters passed through a censor before they were posted. Knowing this, I was careful not to include any information that might prove harmful to our war effort if it got into the wrong hands. I guess I wasn't careful enough, because occasionally comments in my letter would be removed–as was the case in my letter dated March 23.

*Nine o'clock finds me listening to the news in Aunt Lily's home and what encouraging news it is. Our aircraft were all out today, out all last night and probably will be out again tonight. It won't be long now before the allied air forces will have cleaned the skies of enemy fighters. I am looking forward to the time when all raids ——————censored——————will be a piece of* cake then.

My investiture, during which I would be presented with the Distinguished Flying Cross, and that of many other members of the armed forces took place in Buckingham palace on Tuesday, March 21, 1944. Not surprisingly, in a letter home written two days later I described the ceremony.

*After having tea [at the King George and Queen Elizabeth Dominion Officers Club], I borrowed an iron to press my uniform. After all, I was going to meet the king in the morning. I know you will want to know all about the investiture. You probably wish you could have been there to catch a glimpse of your "courageous" son when he marched proudly but rather shakily to receive his "gong" [medal] from the king. I was one of the last to arrive at the palace. Everyone was there bright and early. Waiting to be decorated, we stood in a long queue. We were all in one room; the guests were seated in front and on the sides of the raised platform (dais) on which the king did us the honour of shaking our hand and pinning the "gong" on our chests. I was glad when I found I was not without friends. There were at least five chaps in the queue whom I knew. Four of them were from my old squadron [61 Squadron]. Mac was there as well. One of the boys was in his American uniform. He had ——censored—[probably the missing word was "transferred"] soon after he finished his first tour. Slowly the names were called and at last the RAF began to move. We fooled them. We got hold of some chairs so did not have to stand as long as the others. Trust the RAF to get away with something. No one was supposed to smoke but it took the RAF to determine if the order would be enforced. It was.*

*As we moved closer to the dais I felt a tug on my sleeve. It was Nora [my cousin from Liverpool]. I was surprised; she had not told me she was coming. Unfortunately, she had come rather late and so did not get a good view of the ceremony. One by one we marched up to the dais, turned, bowed [to the king], shook hands, received the "gong," stepped back, bowed, turned right and walked off as proudly as peacocks with a shiny new medal tugging on our left shoulder. I forgot to address the king as "Your Majesty" when he asked me how many sorties I had done. I also forgot to step back when I left the dais. However, no one seemed to notice. Even if they had, they would not have shown any expression of disapproval.*

My father wrote to express his feeling that after the surrender of Italy, the Allies were treating the Italians too generously. In my reply I stated:

*I do not think you are justified in what you say about the manner in which the Allies are treating their former enemy. If we treated them like dogs, they would no doubt treat us as slave drivers. Slave drivers, when they are many times outnumbered and in a strange country, could have a tough time. I would rather see an Italian eating our food than going around knifing our soldiers in the back or acting as spies for the Germans. You see, in order to win this war a bit sooner and so save lives of many of our men, we must have the co-operation of the Italians and the only way we can get that is to do as much as we can to help them. I am not doing my share [in fighting this war] because I want revenge; I am fighting for the betterment of the world. After all, the Allies are not blameless. If they had really done their full share in world affairs, this war would never have begun, Hitler or no Hitler.*

We quickly settled down in our Nissen huts at the Little Staughton air base near Cambridge, which was our home until we completed our tour as pathfinders with 109 Squadron. Cobby and I and the other new members of the squadron were not at all happy with our new home. As I noted in my diary, the aerodrome was

*. . . very dispersed and you should see our hut. Six of us are in one hut and not one locker for the whole lot. I thought Millom was pretty bad but this is a lot worse. Mud everywhere.*

Two days later, I wrote,

*Life is beginning to become normal. The rain shows signs of stopping, so perhaps there will come a time when there is no mud.*

Actually the mud did dry eventually, and we managed to adjust to our surroundings although not without a certain amount of grumbling.

Little Staughton in Hertford County was not far from the village of St. Neots; so, as soon as my bike was found, I cycled there with my fellow officers to enjoy a break away from the base. I was always losing my bike. Perhaps "losing" is not the right word to use. Since I did not have a bike lock, I think airmen were using my bike while I was away and not returning it. It was annoying. But there was not much I could do about it. None of the shops I visited carried bicycle locks.

One evening, Cobby and I had an exciting ride on our bikes. Another officer pulled us to the local pub with his motorcycle. That we enjoyed our cycle rides is indicated by a letter I wrote home.

*After supper the three of us went for a cycle. The weather was very inviting and the scenery was even more so. I have never in Canada seen fields as green as they are over here. The trees have long been in leaf and already you can see the front lawns covered with flowers. We ended up at a dance in the village but before arriving at the village, we met on our way an elderly man who said he was from Canada. For a while I disbelieved him because he had a very broad accent. He went to Canada in 1910 and had lived there until 1939 when he went back to England to see his sister who was very ill. He was a nice sort of chap and we enjoyed his company. It was interesting to hear him talk about old times in England.*

Our hut at Little Staughton

Cobby and I completed twelve ops in April–three to Belgium, five to Germany and the remainder to French targets. We did not mark all of them; some were considered of minor importance so marking was not required for heavy bombers–we bombed them instead. One night we marked two Belgian targets, Tergnier and Ghent, consecutively. While considerable damage was done to railway yards on both these raids, unfortunately in Ghent housing areas were hit, resulting in loss of life and injury.

While our aircraft losses were much lower than we had experienced on 61 Squadron, flying with 109 Squadron did pose some risks. For example an engine failed on one of our aircraft returning from an op. The pilot could not feather the prop, which made it difficult to make an emergency landing on a coastal airfield. Over the North Sea, as the pilot was making his approach, the aircraft turned upside down. The navigator bailed out and was presumed to have drowned. The pilot miraculously righted the plane and made a safe landing. On our return from an OP to Rouen in France on April 19, Cobby experienced difficulty with our landing gear. A warning light on our instrument panel indicated one wheel had not dropped. Since we were landing at about two a.m., the airmen in the control tower could not see well enough to inform us if both wheels were down. Cobby, expecting the worst, made a careful approach and, sure enough, as soon as we hit the "deck" one of our wings touched the ground, bringing us to an abrupt stop.

We noted that many of the targets allocated to us were now ports, military camps, ammunition dumps, railway marshalling yards and major road intersections in France. The targets ranged from Orleans and Le Mans south of Paris to Dieppe, Boulogne and St.Valery on the north coast. This generated rumours of a second front. Presumably the wide area over which Bomber Command targets were chosen was to keep the Germans guessing as to where the attack would be made. This actually proved to be the case. The Allies had established a deception plan in an endeavour to convince the Germans that the Allies would attempt to land their forces along the coast in the Pas de Calais area.

May and June 1944, particularly June, was a hectic period for our squadron. Aircraft were on ops almost every day. Because the targets were usually less than 300 miles from Little Staughton and because of the Mosquito's high-speed capability, the average duration of ops was around two and one-half hours. The ops I made in Lancasters averaged about six and one-half hours.

Our accident and loss rates were also much lower than I had experienced on Lancasters, but we and another crew did have a hair-raising experience. On our return from a raid to mark two targets at St.Valery and Morsalines on the north coast of France, one of our engines failed. While Cobby had no particular difficulty landing, we managed only to turn off the main runway. Consequently, when a Lancaster turned off the runway and started to approach us, we knew we might be in trouble. The Lancaster pilot was at a much higher level than us, so it was doubtful he would see our aircraft in time to avoid a collision. There was nothing Cobby could do. So I got out of our aircraft and by frantically waving a flashlight, I managed to get the attention of the crew in the Lancaster before it rammed into our aircraft.

The near collision was nothing compared to what happened to a Canadian friend, Ernie Garrett, and his pilot on an op on June 2-3 to drop markers on a synthetic oil plant at Leverkusen, near Cologne. The official report of their experience in their heavily damaged aircraft follows:

> 109 PATHFINDER SQUADRON–LITTLE STAUGHTON. 19 Mosquitoes to attack Synthetic Oil Plant, Leverkusen (n. of Cologne) and targets in N. France. MOSQUITO XV1 ML 962–23.28 (hours). F/L A.C. Carter (Capt.) F/O E.W. Garrett (Nav.) Marked with Green TIs [target indicators] from 23,000 ft. A/C badly hit over target. One engine u/s and controls damaged. Hit again at French coast. Crew bailed out over Kent. Both safe.

Our ground crew, 109 Squadron

On crossing the coast of England, Carter was having great difficulty keeping the aircraft stable and concluded that he could not possibly land it safely. Ernie bailed out first through the door directly below him. Carter followed. He landed in a field and was found by a soldier on guard duty. Ernie landed on the roof of the town hall in Caterham, south of London. He hollered for help, but it was three a.m. and whoever heard him must have thought he was a rowdy reveller returning home. Finally after breaking a window he made his way to the ground floor where he found some fire-watchers on night duty, playing cards. With their help, he was able to get to a nearby RAF Station. Eventually, both Ernie and Carter made their way back to Little Staughton and completed their tour of operations together. Unfortunately, there is more to this narration. An eleven month-old baby was killed and his parents injured when a blazing plane crashed on the front garden of a home in Coulsdon. It was Mosquito ML 962.

Back to my letters home, the highlight of which, during May and June, was probably my leave in Edinburgh. While in Edinburgh, I stayed at the North British Station Hotel, which at that time was one of the better hotels in the city. Maybe it still is. Compared to our Nissen hut, it was probably as close to heaven as I could get. For a while, I was concerned that my visit would prove to be dull, but then two persons saved the day:

*You will be wondering how I spent the last part of my leave in Edinburgh. Well, I met a very attractive girl one evening at a dance. Not only was she attractive, she had a pleasant personality. I could have easily fallen for her. Anyway, we spent Thursday, Friday and Saturday nights together. Thursday night, we went to a dance, and Friday night to a variety show starring Ann Shelton, a popular English entertainer and actress. The show as a whole was not very good. One comedian walked off the stage after someone in the audience razzed him. Ann also spent Saturday afternoon with me. We went to a movie and then we spent the remainder of the afternoon in the Princes Street gardens. At the Thursday night dance, I was very surprised to meet one of the naval officers with whom I had spent part of my leave last fall. I had lunch with him and his crewmates on board ship on Sunday. It was a very good meal. Later in the evening I met him again; he was accompanied by his girlfriend, a medical student. She was an interesting person to talk to.*

Sometime later in another letter I had this to say about the war:

*The Italian stalemate has finally ended. The Allies seem to be doing well. For a while I thought the Germans had them stumped. The bomber offensive has been increased still more. Apparently the Americans can now bomb Berlin in daylight with no more trouble than we had when bombing at night. You must think we have not much to show for all this bombing, but wait until the real offensive begins and then we may be all surprised by the number of lives the bombing will have saved. Like you, we all are waiting expectantly for the second front. I feel confident that it will be opened at the proper time so as to risk as few lives as possible. It is worth waiting if, by doing so, we save some lives.*

On June 6, 1944, our target was a coastal battery at Houlgate on the Normandy coast. Takeoff time was 0235 hours. It was D-Day but we did not know it until we had returned to base. We may well have been one of the first aircraft over the Normandy coast. This is what I wrote in my diary:

*It can be said we started D-Day with a bang. The heavies and we in our Mosquitoes bombed gun installations on the coast of Normandy. There was ten-tenths cloud, so we could not see the results. It was breaking day when we returned. American aircraft were already in the air.*

According to subsequent reports, Bomber Command flew over one thousand sorties during the night of June 5-6, most of which supported the invasion forces. It was the task of 109 Squadron to mark many of the targets for the main force which, for the most part, were German rail and road supply routes to battle areas and French ports that sheltered U-boats and small attack vessels.

Eight more ops before leave, four of them aimed at railway terminals and main road intersections in the Normandy area, one at an airfield and the remaining three at flying bomb sites. Because of adverse weather conditions over one of the targets, a recall order was radioed to all participating aircraft. We did not receive the recall, and hence continued to the target. Understandably, on our return we were not very popular for a while with the air control staff and our ground crew because they had to remain on duty until we landed while other personnel could go back to bed.

Back to my letters home. We had learned that the Cooperative Commonwealth Federation had won the election in Saskatchewan.

*We were all somewhat surprised when we learned that the CCF party had won the election in Saskatchewan. I do not know much about the policies of the different parties. I would like to know more. Do you think you could get me the "gen" about the CCF party? Someday I will have to vote, so I would like to know exactly what I am voting for.*

In my letter of July 19, I expressed optimism concerning the role being played by Bomber Command.

*The losses in the RAF have not been as heavy as had been expected, which is a sign that we have gradually obtained mastery of the sky. I suppose you have been reading about our gigantic raids in daylight over France. We are certainly giving the enemy a pounding now. Terry has been over Berlin many times. I believe he has finished his second tour and should be on his way home–that is if he wants to go home. He always was very keen on flying, so he may decide to do a third tour if the RAF will let him.*

I learned later that Terry had actually completed his third tour. He told me later that after returning to Canada he might try to obtain a transfer to Transport Command. He said it was up to other airmen to take his place on bombing operations. My second tour, because I was on pathfinders and probably because we experienced fewer losses, was longer than Terry's.

Many aircrew carried good luck charms. While I did not normally give credence to charms, I may have had second thoughts at one time. In a letter home I referred to a letter from my aunt:

*In it, there was a four-leaf clover that Ann [my teen-aged cousin] had pressed. I carry it with me whenever I fly.*

One of my favourite clubs in London was the Maple Leaf, which had been established for Canadian service personnel. Many of the staff were young Canadian ladies. I liked to talk to them, possibly because their accents took me home. Plus, as stated in my August 10 letter:

*The Canadian girls here are as lovely as ever. They are really a treat for sore eyes. I enjoy talking to them even if I have to dry dishes in order to be in their company long enough to start a conversation.*

As mentioned in my next letter, I did show my appreciation of their company:

*When I left [to return to Little Staughton], as I did before, I bought the girls at the club some flowers.*

While I never managed to date any of the ladies in the club, in the same letter I indicated I did continue to have some success with English ladies:

*Since I have been back [from leave in London], I seem to be busy working or out most nights. Two nights ago, F/O Riley, an English officer, took Mac and me out for the evening in his car. We had dates with three girls from London who are spending their holidays helping farmers with their harvest. I personally do not think they are much help, but anyway the sun does them good and they are away from the buzz bombs.*

Not surprisingly, now that the Allies were concentrating their forces in the Normandy Campaign, many of our bombs and markers were directed at targets that, if successfully bombed, would hinder the movement of German forces. Consequently, we continued to hit railway yards and oil-producing plants, which the Germans needed to fuel transportation vehicles, aircraft, tanks, etc. Also at this time, London was the target of buzz bombs (sometimes referred to V-1 bombs) and V-2 bombs, which had recently been developed by the Germans. While buzz bombs could be destroyed by conventional fighters, rocket-propelled V-2 bombs could not.

On most of our ops in July and August, Cobby and I experienced no particular difficulties. However, danger was always lurking in the skies.

*Last night [July 1] we attacked a target in the Ruhr. We were conned in searchlights for two minutes. Our vapor trails made us a sitting duck.*

While over the target we had not realized that we had been hit by flak. It was only after our ground crew had examined our aircraft that they found a large flak hole in the fuselage behind the wings. We were lucky.

On August 2, we were the lead aircraft of a large number of Lancasters. Our task was to mark a buzz bomb site in France that the Lancasters would bomb. We had never led a formation of Lancasters on a bombing mission before, although we had had some practice flights. To keep within a reasonable lead distance was not easy; Cobby had problems keeping our speed at a level low enough to enable the Lancasters to keep up to us. Our adrenalin was high; we had all these Lancasters in formation depending on us. Suddenly, one of our engines cut, then within seconds, the other engine cut. Cobby signaled me to abandon the aircraft. I reached down to open the door wondering if there would there be any boats in the English Channel to pick me out of the "drink." Then as quickly as they had stopped, the engines began to purr again, first one then the other. But it was too late to carry out our role. The Lancasters had passed over us. Fortunately there was a reserve Mosquito from our squadron, so the bombing took place as planned. Our engines had run out of gas. Cobby had forgotten to switch gasoline tanks.

As we had done in the past, we spent our free time cycling in the country, going to dances in St. Neots, visiting pubs, swimming in the camp pool, and occasionally visiting the three young ladies from London who were helping neighbouring farmers with their harvest. One evening, on our way in Riley's car to visit the girls, the car's motor stopped. We were out of gas. Since gas was rationed there was nothing we could do except to ask a farmer if he could spare a gallon. For some reason I can no longer recollect, Riley suggested that I should approach a farmer who lived only a short distance up a lane. Perhaps he thought my Canadian accent might evoke some sympathy. Still, he could have suggested that Mac knock on the door. Anyway, whatever the reason, I found myself knocking on the farmer's home, as related in my diary:

*A pleasant smile and "Good Evening" were enough to make me forget I was in England. . . . I was surprised to be greeted in such a pleasant fashion when a woman answered my knock. She was able to give us some gas.*

And so we were able to have a pleasant visit with our lady friends. This may have been the night when Mac began to think seriously about Joan. Perhaps had the farmer's wife not given us the gas, the romance between Mac and Joan would not have bloomed into marriage, some months later.

News of the war was encouraging for the most part. There was a rumour going around that the blackout would be lifted from the cities in the north of England and in Scotland. The RAF was losing fewer aircraft. Paris finally was taken, allowing Charles de Gaulle to make his triumphant entry. Unfortunately for Canadians, this heartening news had been offset earlier by the reported murder of nineteen Canadian soldiers by the Germans.

At this time I happily learned of my promotion to flight lieutenant and corresponding salary increase to $8.25 per day. To celebrate, each of us who had been promoted was expected to buy a round of beers for the officers present in the mess. I bought twenty-four pints.

According to my letter home of September 7:

*News for the past few weeks certainly has been encouraging. One by one, former targets of the air forces are being taken by our soldiers. The German air force does not venture out very often now. I do not blame them. They have not a chance. When I arrived in England there were three things I wanted to share with the British–to take part in the second front, to see the lights go on again and to celebrate victory in England. I think my wish will come true. The blackout is to be lifted [over Northern England and Scotland] on the seventeenth, one day after my leave begins.*

We were more relaxed. While fewer aircraft were being shot down or damaged, still there was an element of danger. After we had dropped our markers or bombs depending on the type of op, we experienced an immense feeling of relief as we left the target area and headed for safer skies.

Before my tour came to an end, 109 Squadron lost another aircraft and its crew, and several aircraft were damaged by flak, including ours. It was hit twice during a bombing run. Fortunately the damage was not serious and we returned to base without difficulty. On an op the previous day, after leaving a target in the Ruhr Valley, one of our engines "packed up." My diary entry for September 12 reads:

*The morning and early afternoon were spent in completing an op over the Ruhr. It was a cloudless day. Smoke from yesterday's raid obscured part of the target area. After leaving the target area, one of our engines stopped. For a while I was pretty worried. I expected the other one to "conk out" at any moment.*

Recreation as usual was mostly up to us. There was little organized recreation at any of the bases I had called home. At Little Staughton, we Canadians did try to interest our English friends in softball:

*This week [September 7] we had one game of football and one of softball. The softball game was by far the most enjoyable. Most of the players were English who had only played a few times. I nearly split my sides laughing. Several days later [September 12] three of us spent an evening in a small country pub near here. We took on some farmers in a game of dominoes. They beat us every time. I believe in time I will become accustomed to spending many evenings in such a way. We have had few games of softball in the last few days. I organized one today. The weather was fine. The grass was not wet with dew as it sometimes is. The pilots against the navigators. They were thoroughly beaten.*

Presumably, in the latter part of 1944, I felt that I would survive the war. I began to look to the future with more confidence. What would I do when I was posted back to Canada? Would I volunteer for further military service in the Far East? Would I leave the armed forces? What then? Would I buy a farm with my savings or would I try to obtain a university degree? That I finally made a decision is confirmed in my letter home written on October 19.

*A whole night of work ahead of me. I hate these irregular hours and certainly will be a happy man when I can once more have a full night's sleep every night. I have not been doing as much flying these past few days as I had hoped I would. I believe it will be touch and go for me to be home by Christmas–that is, if I am sent home. I have gone over the points carefully for and against going home, and have come to the conclusion that, if I will lose anything by going home, it will be very little. I have made up my mind to attend university, that is, if it is possible for me to get into the University of Toronto. I have five subjects I will have to pass before I will be allowed to enter. I have also made up my mind to go "halfers" with you to buy Britton's farm. I believe that you, Dad, will have no trouble keeping your job but then there are Harold [my brother], Sam and Joe [my cousins] to think about. Once I get into university, if I ever do under the governmental support scheme, my worries will be over. I am quite confident that I can make the grade.*

Now that I was near the end of my second tour and would likely be repatriated, I made special efforts to visit my relatives, including my brother Harold, who had arrived in England recently with the RCAF. I also wanted to visit Wallace, my Bobcaygeon friend, and another mutual friend who were both with an RCAF squadron near Darlington in Yorkshire. However, I had had my fill of travelling in crowded trains and decided that this time I would hitchhike. According to my diary entry for October 27, luck was with me:

*I left camp at 0930 hours with Cobby in his car. I caught a lift in a lorry just as I stepped out of the car. Later I got another lift in a lorry bound for Glasgow. I was lucky. When we stopped for petrol, I was offered a lift to Darlington. I have been on the road for eight hours. I will not try to locate Wallace tonight. I may go to a dance.*

My average travelling speed was twenty-five miles per hour. Not very good. I could have made better time by train. Still, according to a letter I wrote home on November 1, I enjoyed the trip:

*All my lifts were in large trucks. They were not very comfortable but I found the change interesting. For once I was able to see the country I was passing through. [Standing in the aisle of a passenger car on a train did not afford a good view of the passing countryside.] Wallace had not received my letter. As fate would have it, he was on his day off. However, Bruce Stinson [another Bobcaygeon friend] was easy to find. [Two days later, Wallace was given another day off.] By bus and by train we spent some time in three towns. We went through the Durham Cathedral in the afternoon. Later we went to see what turned out to be a very good movie. After supper we attended a dance that reminded me of the Palais in Nottingham–that is, the girls did. Hundreds of them and beautiful, too. We ate very well. We had chicken twice. I managed in one of the towns to use my coupons to get Wallace a pair of shoes.*

At camp, as before my leave, operational flying never ceased with aircraft taking off at all hours except when the weather was unfavourable. We were not the only crews in the air. Americans in their Flying Fortresses took off on daylight raids, often to the same targets we had attacked the night before. One day one of the Fortresses dropped in, literally. The crew, for reasons unknown to me, had bailed out leaving the Fortress to eventually crash. It actually crashed on our airfield and, as I said in my diary, *blew up to smithereens*. Fortunately, no one at Little Staughton was injured by the blast of the exploding aircraft.

In late evening on October 23, we participated in a thousand-bomber raid over Essen. This raid was not considered successful, at least according to my diary. There was too much cloud cover. Subsequent reports on this raid and a second raid to Essen a day later indicate that the raids did actually inflict considerable damage. Essen continued to be attacked, with the last major night raid occurring on December 13-14. However, on March 11, 1945, over a thousand RAF aircraft were involved in a daylight raid. Altogether, Essen had been bombed more than sixty times by the RAF. It should be noted that it was also a target of American bombers. Because losses generally were high over Essen, I was fortunate in that I was called only three times to take part on ops over that city.

My last op of my second tour and of the war, as far as I was concerned, took place on November 4, 1944, to Bochum, a small city in the same general area as Essen. Seven hundred and forty- nine aircraft were involved. Twenty-eight aircraft, none of them Mosquitoes, were lost. My diary entry made on the day after the raid follows:

*Last night saw me finish my second tour with an op to Bochum in the Ruhr. The raid, I believe, was successful.*

Martin Middlebrook and Chris Everitt in their book, *The Bomber Command Diaries* (1990), state:

> . . . the attack based upon standard pathfinder marking techniques was particularly successful. Severe damage was caused to the centre of Bochum. More than 4000 buildings were destroyed or seriously damaged; 980 Germans and 14 foreigners were killed. Bochum's industrial areas were also severely damaged, particularly the important steel works. This was the last major raid by Bomber Command on this target.

Writing home a few days after the Bochum raid, I informed my parents that I had completed my second tour. I imagine they were happy to know that I would now be coming home and had escaped the war unscathed.

*The boys are making such a racket that I do not think I will be able to concentrate on this letter. If it is short, that will be the reason.*

*I returned from leave without any adventures worth noting. I had to wait two hours in town for a lift back to camp. I managed while I was waiting to get a reasonable meal, the first I had had since breakfast. At camp I found that a number of the boys had caught up to me in the number of operations they had done. Some had finished [their tours]. Mac and I finished together four nights ago. For a while I hardly realized that I had finished. I kept thinking my name would be on the flying list. Now I have gotten over that and feel very relieved. I only wish I could be sure that I will not have to wait too long to return to Canada. I know it will be at least three weeks before I am put on board a boat. I am quite certain now that I will return to Canada.*

*While waiting for a posting to a repatriation depot, I am going on two weeks' leave. I am going to spend a few days in Nottingham and the remainder in and around London. I may see Aunt Bessie for a few days. Harold thinks he will get a week's leave this weekend. I have written him asking him to meet me in London. I am not sure as to whether he will get my letter in time. I have promised the people [Herb and Doris Winfield, the farming couple, and several others] I know near Oxford that I would spend a few days with them. I would also like to visit the station [Upper Heyford] at which I spent a year as a student bomb-aimer and later as an instructor.*

I did meet Harold and was able to make the other visits. Harold, I believe, was becoming a bit disgruntled with the air force. After all, he had expected to be spending time in the air by now, not sitting around with little to do. I promised him that when I was repatriated, I would ship my bike to him so at least he could go for rides in countryside as I had done when I was feeling in the doldrums.

# CHAPTER 11

## *Repatriation*

I spent my leave as planned and received my posting to Warrington, the repatriation camp. My November 23 diary entry reads as follows:

*I spent all day getting cleared. I sent Harold the five parcels I had received. This evening I spent some time in the mess with the boys. I wonder if I shall ever meet any of them again. They are not a bad lot and have been very good to me.*

Of them all, I only met Mac again. In fact I have seen him several times at his home in Edmonton. He did marry Joan, one of the volunteer farm helpers, and eventually became a dentist. I occasionally think of all the other friends I left behind, particularly Cobby. I don't suppose I would recognize any of them if I did meet them. Fifty-five years can create havoc with our bodies. Plus some of them will have passed on.

The day after my arrival at Warrington, as noted in my diary entry,

*. . . saw everyone I was supposed to see this morning. There are sixty-six beds in our hut. We will live like recruits.*

Possibly someone in authority realized that we should have better accommodation, so we were moved to another camp. Unfortunately, the meals there were awful.

I wrote my last letter home from England on November 22, 1944. It was my 120th letter. While I was in England, my parents wrote me 168 letters, which was over four letters a month, and they sent me seventy-five parcels. Thinking back, I realize how important those letters and parcels were. Receiving letters on a regular basis did a lot to boost my morale. Also, replying to their letters helped me to cope, and to fill in the empty hours between ops. Of course, I received many other letters from my grandparents, other relatives, and friends.

On December 1, we boarded a train to start us on our journey home:

*Spent most of the day studying and writing letters. Also had a few games of snooker and table tennis. We left camp at nine p.m. for the first part of our journey home. The station band gave us a sendoff. I think we will be traveling most of the night, as it is rumoured we sail from Greenock. This train ride will certainly be a bind. The following morning we arrived at Greenock at four-thirty. It was eight-thirty before we got on board the ship, the Queen Elizabeth. What a ship it is. I can hardly realize I am not on land. We had a wonderful breakfast, a fruit cocktail followed by porridge or corn flakes, then an egg and bacon. All other meals were good. I have borrowed a book by Bret Hart so I am well away.*

In the evening the crew pulled up anchor three years less sixteen days since my arrival in Greenock. Sailing on the *Queen Elizabeth* was a far cry from our outward voyage from Halifax. Even though the sea was not nearly as rough, a number of my mates felt a bit queasy. The food was so good it would have taken more than a queasy feeling to keep me out of the dining room. Not surprisingly, we were not treated as passengers would have been treated in more peaceful times. Two other officers and I shared a cabin that, due to the blackout, was uncomfortably hot and stale. I spent a lot of time playing cards with my mates, reading, studying geometry or algebra, or occasionally just sitting on the deck whenever the sun brought the temperature to a comfortable level. Fortunately, there was an orchestra on board that put on a concert for us one evening.

Returning armed force personnel were not the only passengers. Young British wives of servicemen were on their way to start a new life in Canada. A baby was born to one of them. I sometimes wonder about that baby. Was it a girl or boy and what was its future?

As recorded in my diary entry for December 8:

*This morning soon after breakfast, land was sighted. Long Island, someone said. After that I kept on the lookout most of the time, as I did not want to miss anything, especially the Statue of Liberty. We docked at one in the afternoon. At seven we left the QE. I was anxious to have a few hours in New York, as the neon signs were quite inviting.*

Not surprisingly, we didn't get any time in New York–understandably, because had we been let loose, we would have been very hard to control. As it was we were directed onto a train bound for Ottawa. By mid-morning the following day, we were formally welcomed home by the Hon. Angus Lewis MacDonald, acting minister for Air, and a large crowd of Ottawa residents. After reporting to the Rockcliffe airport, we had a few hours to visit Ottawa and Hull before boarding our train for Toronto.

Home at last, at least to the small apartment my parents were renting on College Street. I was surprised to see my parents and my brother, Frank, in the crowd waiting at the station as I had not informed them of my expected arrival. Almost four weeks' leave ahead of me. What was I going to do? My first move following a reunion with my parents and Frank was to call on an RCAF education officer to apply for correspondence courses in two of the subjects–physics and algebra–I would need for admission to university. Next I visited the University of Toronto for information on enrolment requirements. I wanted to be sure that if and when I had obtained senior matriculation, I could count on being accepted as a student.

A few days later I went to visit a cousin in Buffalo. It was there I purchased my first wristwatch for $47, which I still wear occasionally. A visit to Bobcaygeon followed, where I was moved by a reception arranged for me by Tom Martin, a well-known farmer and the father of my friend Wallace. I had no difficulty hitchhiking back to Toronto in time to enjoy Christmas with my parents. Boxing Day found on my way again, this time to Neepawa and Minnedosa, Manitoba, to spend the next few days with my grandparents and my aunt and her family. What I remember most about this visit was the New Year's bash with Aunt Glady and Uncle Morris:

*New Year's Eve was spent this year at Aunt Glady's. It is the best start I have made in a new year since I have been in the air force. What a dinner! A huge turkey and everything that goes with it. In the evening Aunt Glady and I went to church. Later the three of us are going out to celebrate. Just before twelve, the three of us and a lot of Aunt Glady's friends entered the dance hall. A few minutes later I was having my first dance in Canada and with Aunt Glady. We stayed at the dance until it ended at three. We all met again where we were able to indulge ourselves with more food. At five I climbed into bed.*

Soon after I had returned to Toronto, I received notice of my posting to Fingal, a holding station for returning aircrew. We did not have any allotted tasks and for the most part we had to depend on our own initiative to keep occupied. Fingal was crowded. There was no accommodation available for many of us, so another officer and I rented a room in the nearby town of St.Thomas, where I had no difficulty putting in time. I did a lot of studying on the two correspondence courses and my roommate and I enrolled in a typing course. As far as I can recall, we were the only men taking the course. While I was at Fingal, seventy officers received their discharge from the air force. I expected mine to come any day, but it didn't. Instead I received four days' leave.

Back in Toronto, I visited the Ontario Rehabilitation School:

*This morning [February 8] I went down to the Ontario Rehabilitation School as I have decided that is where I will spend the next few months. I am fed up living day after day not knowing what is going to happen to me.*

On February 12, I managed to get an unauthorized posting to Toronto, and confident of my imminent discharge, I started studying full time. But the air force authorities were not through with me yet. On February 26, after being recalled to Fingal, I was told I was being posted to Trenton, Ontario, and then three hours later I was told I was posted to the St. Johns air base in Quebec. According to a diary entry for that day,

*Although I tried my best to persuade the authorities to let me retire, they would not play.*

I now had no choice but to carry on with the correspondence courses I had already started and move to St. Johns.

There I flew twice as a screen navigator before learning of my posting to Rivers, Manitoba, to take a special five-week instructor's course:

*March 10. Arrived at Rivers at four-thirty p.m. It has changed a lot since I was here in '41. Our course will last five weeks. Our chief instructor thinks we will all be put to work as soon as we finish. It is*

*certainly a change to get out in the wide-open spaces. From the window of my room I can see for miles. March 17. Gave my first lecture here. Do not think I did too badly. This evening I attended a dance in our mess. I had a fair time but my respect for Canadian girls has dropped a little. A few days ago I was made class senior. The boys on the whole like me I think, which pleases me.*

While taking the course I continued to work on physics and algebra, usually studying two to three hours every evening while in camp and not flying. Upon completion of the course on April 10, we were again considered for posting to other air force stations. Navigators who had only completed one tour of operations overseas were asked to volunteer for a second tour. Ten days passed before we received details of our postings. I had hoped to go to the west coast, as that was a part of Canada I had yet to see, but I wasn't posted anywhere. Instead, one other officer and I would stay in Rivers. Then on April 12, 1945, President Franklin Roosevelt died: *Roosevelt's death today no doubt shocked most of the world. Fate apparently stepped in and said we would have no Roosevelt at the San Francisco conference [called to write the charter of the proposed United Nations]. His death may change the whole outcome of this war. I think he would have done much to ensure a lasting peace. He is a politician I respected.*

Soon two of us were paired to assume responsibility for a new class of trainees, including lecturing to the trainees and flying with them. I was in the air almost every second day as screen navigator. For the most part, I enjoyed the flights, probably because the pilots would occasionally let me take over the controls. Actually, I had always wanted to be a pilot, and so I was always pleased to take over.

There was not a lot to do in our spare time at Rivers. Occasionally there would be a dance, but for the most part we were left to our own devices. A few of us would sometimes go horseback riding or play softball. Luckily for me, I had my relatives at Minnedosa and Neepawa whom I could visit whenever I had an opportunity.

On May 7, we heard the news we all had been waiting for:

*At last the European War has ended. No longer will mothers and sweethearts of boys overseas have to worry about their welfare. We who remain alive, out of those who went over with us, realize how much we have to be thankful for. I don't know why I was allowed to live when others died. For the privilege of living I shall devote my life to the welfare of others.* (My intentions were good but I can't say I lived up to them.)

With the declaration of the Peace, I would much rather have been in London. How could we celebrate at Rivers, a tiny community? About the only way was to drink a bit more and be merry, which was what I think everyone did but the commanding officer. He kept his cool.

Fellow officers at Rivers

*May 14–Twenty-four years old. When I was going to school I thought at twenty-four I'd know all I wanted to know, but now I realize I will never know enough.*

And so my birthday passed and life continued. I passed the algebra exam and started the high school trigonometry course. This with the physics course that I was still working on would take care of a lot of my free time. I did manage, however, to spend a weekend with my aunt and her family in Regina. About this time I was pleased to learn that Harold was now home from overseas and would soon leave the air force.

Our class of trainees was large, at least until those trainees who had not volunteered for service in the Far East were discharged early in July. Morale was a bit low around camp. We wondered what the future held for us. With the European war over, there was no need for many new navigators. Obviously, the time was coming when our services would no longer be required. We could receive our discharge at any time. But not for me.

On August 7, I was posted to Toronto to take an administration course. Shortly before my departure, I completed the trigonometry course and wrote the mid-term physics exam.

With many other officers, some of whom I knew, I had no trouble settling in to being a student again, although I wondered why I was taking the course when the end of the Far East war appeared imminent. I had been on the course only six days, when we heard the news on August 14:

*Japan surrendered today. News came at eight p.m. I stopped work on the spot. Sam [my cousin and a soldier] and I spent most of the night downtown making fools of ourselves, but there were many others making even bigger fools of themselves. It was five a.m. before we got to bed. We did not spend one cent on our celebrations. August 16–Back to work again. It seems rather silly to be taking a course when the war is over. When we were drilling this morning, someone in a car hollered that the war was over. I am putting in two hours of study this evening. It is difficult to study when it is so easy to go out and have a night's fun.*

In the classroom and on the parade ground, we were concerned as to what would happen to us, which I expressed in my diary on August 23:

*Now that war is really and truly over, rumours are beginning to be spread again in the air force. None of them I think have any foundation so I try to ignore them as much as possible.*

Actually, it was an unsettling period for us; we expected to learn any time soon that our services were no longer required. I again made enquires at U of T to ensure I would have a reasonable chance of enrolling in a university course should I obtain the required credits. The fateful day finally arrived on August 30.

*Learned this afternoon that I have been discharged from the air force. Now I can settle down and try to realize a few of my ambitions. I am leaving tomorrow for Rivers, where I will start going through the discharge procedure.*

I was given a whole week and so had time to visit Minnedosa and Neepawa. On my return to Toronto, I contacted the Rehabilitation College to ensure that I would be allowed to enrol. However, it was not until September 20 when I finally become a civilian, never to wear a uniform again. Two days before, Group Captain Denton Massey, on behalf of the air force, gave us a farewell speech and then shook hands with each of us.

# CHAPTER 12

## *World Without War*

It would be inappropriate for me, a survivor of World War II, to end my story without an expression of concern for the future of the world. As a veteran, I don't want my children and your children, and future generations to live in a world in which disputes are settled by war. I have seen enough of the horrors of war to convince myself there must be other ways to solve the problems between nations and within nations that have in the past led to war.

While we, the peoples of the world, may never be able to prevent conflicts from occurring from time to time, surely we can take steps to ensure that these conflicts do not escalate into a world war–a war from which mankind might not survive. Slowly, very slowly, old beliefs on national destiny and absolute sovereignty are fading away. But will they fade away quickly enough to allow the removal of barriers to peaceful solutions of the many problems facing countries before they are caught on the path that leads to conflict? Our goal and that of succeeding generations should be the eventual removal of these barriers.

It is time we looked upon the world as our world. Problems affecting the well being of people wherever they may live can no longer be ignored. With the weaponry now available, conflicts on the distant side of the earth could directly involve us. It is imperative that we become more concerned with the management of the world; we need to view the world as we view our country. Problems arising from more sophisticated weaponry and trade in weapons must be tackled and solved. There are, of course, other problems not directly concerned with war that must be tackled; otherwise they too could lead to war.

Shipments of small arms are being made by weapons manufacturers to countries experiencing internal conflicts in which many people are being killed. Logically it can be assumed that fewer people would be killed if they did not have recourse to these modern weapons. Nor is it as likely that internal conflicts would break out as often as they do now if weapons were not readily available. But by far the greatest threat to the world is not military exports; it is the thousands of nuclear weapons that are held by nuclear weapon countries. As noted in the May '99 newsletter of Peacefund Canada:

> *The New England Journal of Medicine*, the most prestigious journal of its kind, recently published a study that examines the impact of an accidental nuclear strike from a single Russian submarine; 6.3 million people would be dead in the first half hour. The ballooning catastrophe that would result from likely US retaliation cannot be imagined.

Besides the serious problem of production and trade in weapons, there are the problems arising from global climatic change and excessive population growth, which could result in increasing hardships that in turn could lead to conflicts within and between nations.

The problems as noted above are world problems. Therefore they and other problems encompassing the world must be solved by world institutions. The United Nations (UN) was established in 1945 for such a purpose, but unfortunately it does have some shortcomings that hinder its ability to solve these problems. These deficiencies must be addressed if the UN is to effectively fulfill its mandate. **It is imperative**. Otherwise all the lives lost in World War II and prior wars will have been wasted. As noted in my diary on January 18, 1942, I had hoped World War II would bring peace.

*If I should pass on before this war is over I will leave this world with one small regret, the regret that I will not be able to help, with those I love, in my small way, to make this war bring peace and happiness to the world as it once only brought tragedy, sorrow and despair.*

The UN must be democratized. Reform of the most powerful body–the Security Council–to make it more representative of the world's nations and the removal of its veto would go a long way to making the UN more responsive to world problems. Also to ensure it can fulfill its mandate, the UN must have adequate financial resources. In addition, I would hope that the UN would take steps to improve its peace operations. The crisis in Rwanda was not the first, but perhaps the most glaring example of the failure of the UN to intervene quickly in order to prevent conflict. The International Court of Justice needs to be strengthened. It currently has jurisdiction only when the states involved agree to abide by its decision.

I hope that the lives lost in wars will not be in vain and that the UN will be able to stop conflicts from starting, or at least stop them from spreading to other nations. There will be more than enough problems to solve to ensure the peoples of the world can live in harmony and enjoy meaningful lives.

As Shridath Ramphal, former secretary-general of the Commonwealth Nations, said in his book *Our Country, The Planet,* "We know what can be done. We have the means to do it. Can we muster the will, all governments, all societies, all people, to take the path of enlightened change?"

# EPILOGUE

Considering its size, Bomber Command suffered more casualties than any other unit of the armed forces under the control of British and Commonwealth governments–over 47,000 aircrew died on operations, over 9,700 were taken prisoner and 8,400 were injured or wounded while undergoing training or on operations. The magnitude of these losses is obvious when their numbers are compared to the overall number of aircrew in Bomber Command–110,000.

Were these losses warranted in relation to the damage done in enemy territory? The War Office had no choice but to commence a bombing offensive. First, the British people were being bombarded by the Luftwaffe with devastating effects. Second, the Russians were expecting a second front. The British had no option but to commence a large-scale bombing campaign, which the Americans eventually joined. The bombing undoubtedly forced the Germans to deploy a large number of armed force personnel to man anti-aircraft batteries and searchlights in targeted areas. Even though many bombs missed their targets, not all of them did. As a result, traffic on railways and roads was disrupted, oil production was reduced and, in some cases munitions, armament and power plants were knocked out. Bombers successfully destroyed V-1 and V-2 sites, whose bombs were having a demoralizing effect on Londoners. Coupled with the mines laid in harbours to hinder German shipping, the bombing may well have shortened the war and saved the lives of countless civilians and service personnel on both sides.

I regret that we had had no choice but to go to war. Hitler had to be stopped. If he had been left to his own devices, think what would have happened. His belief in the superiority of the Aryan race would have continued to bring about untold suffering and bloodshed. However, what bothers me is that so many fine young men lost their lives. Men who were my comrades, who shared my joys, my hopes and inspirations, men whom I respected and who would have played worthwhile roles in life had they had been allowed to live as I have. I survived because I was lucky. Perhaps that four-leaf clover given to me by my young cousin, Ann, which I kept in the pocket of my battle dress, may have helped.

I did graduate from the University of Toronto in 1949 with a degree in mining geology and began what proved to be a successful career with industry and government.

I am grateful for the opportunities that my fallen friends and comrades made possible through their sacrifice.

# APPENDIX

*Friends Who were Killed in Action–May 1942 to October 1943*

***Baird, David Munroe***, from St. John's, Newfoundland. Lost his life May 31, 1942, age 20. While returning from the first 1,000-Bomber Raid, which took place over Cologne, Germany, his pilot lost control of the Wellington bomber aircraft over the North Sea and Munroe bailed out as ordered. The pilot regained control and was able to bring the aircraft back to its base near Oxford. All other members of the crew had not had time to bail out and thus survived to fly again. Baird has no known grave; his name is inscribed on the Runnymede War Memorial, Surrey, England.

***Le Blanc, Charles Emile,*** from Belle Cote, Inverness County, Nova Scotia. Killed in action June 17, 1942, age 19. Target: Essen. The starboard engine of the Wellington failed and Le Blanc was forced to jettison the bomb load in an attempt to maintain altitude and return to base. The aircraft could not get above 3,000 feet and was shot down over the heavily defended city of Antwerp, Belgium. Le Blanc maintained control long enough for his crew to bail out; he, however, waited too long and went down with the aircraft. Two of the crew were taken prisoners of war, while the other two Canadian crewmembers evaded capture and returned safely to England. Le Blanc is buried in the Canadian War Cemetery, Adegem, East Flanders, Belgium.

***Mosher, Paul Darby***, from Halifax, Nova Scotia. Killed in action July 10, 1942, age 20. Whitley aircraft failed to return from operations. Mosher has no known grave; his name is inscribed on the Runnymede Memorial.

***Madson, John Emmett***, from Winnipeg, Manitoba. Killed in action August 20, 1942, age 20. Second pilot on a sea patrol operation over the Bay of Biscay. Interred in the Bilbao British Cemetery, Lujua, Spain.

***Aleo, Joseph***, from Niagara Falls, Ontario, age 21.

***Dewar, Duncan Hugh Alexander***, from Oyama, British Columbia, age 22.

***Phair, Maurice Andrew***, from Limestone, Maine, USA, age 24.

These three airmen were killed on January 13, 1943, when their Lancaster was shot down at Dusseldorf during a bombing operation over Essen. All are buried in the Reichswald Forest War Cemetery at Rheinburg, Germany.

***Bird, Robert Francis***, from Calgary, Alberta. Killed in action January 16, 1943, age 22. Target Berlin. The Lancaster was shot down in a suburb of Berlin at Döberitz. All members of the crew were killed. Bird is buried in the Berlin War Cemetery, Charlotteburg, Germany.

***Hamann, Charles William***, from Hamilton, Ontario. Killed in action October 26, 1943, age 23. Number 160 Burma Squadron Liberator failed to return from a photo reconnaissance mission over Nicobar Island in the Adaman Sea. Hamann has no known grave. His name is inscribed on the Singapore War Memorial.

# BIBLIOGRAPHY

Longmate, N. 1988. *The bombers*. Tiptree, Essex: Anchor Brendon Limited.

Middlebrook, M. and Everitt, C. 1990. *The Bomber Command diaries*. Markham, Ontario: Penguin Books Canada Ltd.

Ramphal, S. 1992. *Our country, the planet*. Washington, DC: Island Press.

Allison, L. and Hayward, H. (n.d.) *They shall grow not old.* Brandon, Manitoba: The Commonwealth Air Training Plan Museum Inc.

## ABOUT THE AUTHOR

John Patterson was born in Medicine Hat, Alberta, in 1921. At that time and for the next eight years, his father taught in public schools in southwestern Saskatchewan. In 1929, his parents purchased farmland in that area and began what proved to be a very precarious way to make a living. The Depression took its toll, and in 1937 John and his family pulled up stakes to move to a farm near Bobcaygeon, Ontario.

Schooling was not an easy proposition for John, who had to walk 7.2 kilometres each way to school every day; but he did manage to obtain his junior matriculation, and one year later was hitchhiking to Toronto to join the RCAF.

Following his service in the RCAF, John attended the University of Toronto, graduating in 1949 as a mining geologist. There followed an interesting and rewarding career as an employee of various mining companies, the British Columbia mines department, and the departments of Mines and Technical Services (now Natural Resources) and of Industry in Ottawa.

In his retirement, John has been a supporter and active member of several organizations whose ultimate goal is the elimination of war as a means of settling disputes between nations.